AN-NAWAWI'S FORTY HADITH

Translated by
Ezzedin Ibrahim & Denys Johnson-Davies

AN-NAWAWI'S

FORTY HADITH

AN ANTHOLOGY OF THE SAYINGS OF
THE PROPHET MUHAMMAD

TRANSLATED BY

EZZEDDIN IBRAHIM

B.A. (Cairo); Ph. D. (Lond.)

DENYS JOHNSON-DAVIES
(ABDULWADOUD)
M. A. (Cantab.)

**IN THE NAME OF ALLAH
THE MERCIFUL THE COMPASSIONATE**

Dar Al Taqwa Ltd. **January 2010**
ISBN 978-1-870582-77-3

All rights reserved. No part of this publication may be reproduced, stored in a retrieval system, or transmitted, in any form or by any means, electronic, mechanical, photocopying, recording or otherwise, without the prior permission of the publishers.

Selected and translated by
Ezzeddin IBRAHIM
Denys Johnson-DAVIES

Produced with special permission of the translator.

Published by:
Dar Al Taqwa Ltd.
7A Melcombe Street
Baker Street
London NWI 6AE

Website : www.daraltaqwaonline.com
E-Mail : info@daraltaqwaonline.com

Printed by:
IMAK Offset Printing Center
www.imakofset.com.tr
isa@imakofset.com.tr

Contents

	Page
Introduction by the translators in English	7
Introduction by the translators in English	12
Imām an-Nawawī's Introduction in arabic with English translation	18
The Hadith : Arabic text with facing English translation	26

In the name of Allah the Merciful
the Compassionate

INTRODUCTION

There are two main sources for an understanding of Islam: the Holy Qur'ān and the collections of the recorded words, actions and sanctions of the Prophet Muḥammad which make up the *sunna* and which are normally referred to as Hadith.

As the Holy Qur'ān is the word of Allah it must be strictly followed; in the same way the teachings contained in the Prophet's *sunna* must be observed by all who profess to be Muslims, for about them the Holy Qur'ān says: "And whatsoever the Messenger giveth you, take it. And whatsoever he forbiddeth, abstain (from it)."

Thus the *sunna,* in the form of Hadith, is complementary to the Holy Book itself: it helps to explain and clarify the Holy Qur'ān and to present practical applications of its teachings. Without a study of Hadith a Muslim's knowledge of his faith remains incomplete, and without it the non-Muslim is unable to form a true picture of the Islamic faith and its fundamental spiritual, moral, legislative, and cultural principles.

Previous translations of Hadith into English

While many attempts have been made to render the meanings of the Holy Qur'ān into English, much less attention has been given to the Hadith of the Prophet Muḥammad. Apart from various short selections of Hadith that have

appeared in English translation in various parts of the Islamic world, notably in Pakistan and India, the following are, to the best of the translators' knowledge, the most important attempts:
1. A translation of Mishkāt al-Maṣābīḥ, a selection compiled by Walī ad-Dīn Muḥammad ibn 'Abdullah al-Khaṭīb at-Tabrīzī (died 737 A.H.), undertaken by A.N. Matthews. The translation appeared in two volumes (Calcutta 1809/10); it has long been out of print and copies of it are scarce. Some of the Hadith included in the Mishkat do not appear in the translation.
2. Another translation of Mishkāt al-Maṣābīḥ entitled 'The Hadis', undertaken by Al-Haj Maulana Fazlul Karim. It appeared in four volumes (Calcutta 1938), together with the Arabic text. The translator has taken some liberties in the arrangement of the text and has added to it certain other selections of Hadith taken from al-Ghazālī's 'Iḥyā' 'ulūm ad-Dīn'. The translation does nevertheless include the complete contents of the Mishkāt and retains its general form.
3. A part of the Ṣaḥīḥ of al-Bukhārī undertaken by the Austrian Muslim, Muḥammad Asad, together with the Arabic text. The translation began appearing in sections in Lahore in 1938 and was unhappily discontinued.
4. A new and complete translation of Mishkāt al-Maṣābīḥ made by Dr. James Robson, Professor of Arabic at Manchester University, in four volumes (Lahore 1965, and reprinted in 1973).
5. A complete translation of Muslim's Ṣaḥīḥ made by 'Abdul Ḥamīd Ṣiddīqī, which has appeared in four volumes (Lahore 1973).
6. A new translation of al-Bukhārī's Ṣaḥīḥ, which has begun to appear under the imprint of the Islamic University

in Medina and is being undertaken by Dr. Muḥammad Muḥsin Khān. The translation will be in four volumes and includes the Arabic text.

While these translations go some way towards providing satisfactory renderings in English of the Prophet's *sunna,* they do inevitably contain the occasional shortcoming both in a proper understanding of the Arabic text and in providing an English rendering that is faithful to the original and linguistically acceptable. The present translators thus believe that there is still scope for further attempts in this field.

A method of translation

Translation is at best a difficult task, especially from languages as different in grammar, syntax and cultural background as Arabic and English. The difficulties are further increased when the task to hand is that of rendering into English a religious work such as the present one. In translating the Hadith of the Prophet it is clearly necessary that the translator be possessed of such a breadth and depth of knowledge of the Arabic and English languages, together with a full understanding of the Islamic faith in all its aspects, as are most unlikely to be found in a single person. Recognising this fact, it was felt that the obvious solution was for such translations to be undertaken by two persons working in close collaboration; two persons whose academic backgrounds would both overlap and complement each other. The translation of the present small volume of Hadith has been undertaken by a procedure of work in which each translator has his own particular role and at the same time acts as a check on the other.

The choice of an-Nawawī's 'Forty Hadith', selected

by Imām Yaḥyā ibn Sharaf ad-Dīn an-Nawawī (died 676 A.H.) as the first work on which to try out this method was dictated by the fact that since its compilation in the 13th century A.D. this collection has enjoyed widespread acceptance by Muslims as a work that, despite its modest size, incorporates a comprehensive selection of well-authenticated Hadith on the most important aspects of religious knowledge.

The translators hope to follow up the present volume with a further and more comprehensive book of Hadith, also compiled by the Imām an-Nawawī, entitled Riyāḍ aṣ-Ṣālıḥīn ('The Gardens of the Godly').

Some points about the translation

1.) Where a Hadith includes a verse from the Holy Qur'ān the translators have used the translation of the English Muslim, Marmaduke Pickthall, from his 'The Meaning of the Glorious Koran'.

2.) Every care has been taken to ensure the accuracy of the translation. In instances where a freer rendering would have sounded more effective, we have sacrificed effect for accuracy. Where a literal translation was unacceptable and we have felt obliged to add words to the translation, such words have been enclosed in square brackets.

3.) It will be found that certain Arabic words which are of a religious nature and are peculiar to Islam, such as *īmān*, *iḥsān* and *zakāt* have been retained in their Arabic form and explanatory notes given to them. In the case of *Ḥadīth*, often rendered by Orientalists as Tradition, it was decided to retain the Arabic word. As it occurs throughout the work it has not been supplied with the distinguishing marks required by the rules of transliteration and we have simply spelt it 'Hadith'. Furthermore, the word has been treated as a collective noun.

On the question of whether to translate *Allah* as God or retain the word in its Arabic form, we decided on the word *Allah* because it is in general use amongst Muslims, whether or not they are speaking Arabic. Were it not for this consideration the word *Allah* would have been rendered as God.

4.) Proper names and words retained in Arabic have been transliterated in accordance with the usual method followed by scholars of Arabic, except of course with words such as Caliph which have become part of the English language.

5.) The notes have been kept to a minimum, being supplied only when it was necessary to a proper understanding of the English translation, to explain some term, to provide background information, or to point out where the translators have departed in small measure from the Arabic text.

6.) It will be seen that each Hadith consists of two parts: a.) the *sanad*, or chain of authorities, through which the Hadith was transmitted and which an-Nawawī gives in a much abbreviated form, and b.) the *matn*, or text of the Hadith. Finally, the compiler indicates the original collection or collections from which he has taken the Hadith.

In conclusion, it is hoped that this small book may contribute to an understanding of Hadith and that it will encourage English language readers to extend their knowledge of this literature.

The translators

بِسْمِ اللَّهِ الرَّحْمَنِ الرَّحِيمِ

مقدِّمَة المترجمِين

الحمد لله ، والصلاة والسلام على رسول الله ، وعلى آله وصحبه ومن والاه ، وبعد .

فإن مصدري الإسلام الرئيسين ، اللذَيْن يُعوَّل عليهما في فهم تعاليمه ، وهديه في أمور الدين والدنيا ، هما القرآن الكريم والسنة النبوية المطهرة . فالأول هو كلام الله الذي ﴿ **لا يأتيه الباطل من بين يديه ولا من خلفه ، تنزيل من حكيم حميد** ﴾ . والثاني هو توجيه النبي صلى الله عليه وسلم الواجب الاتباع ﴿ **وما آتاكم الرسولُ فخذوه ، وما نهاكم عنه فانتهوا** ﴾ .

والسنة هي شارحة القرآن الكريم ، ومتممة هديه بما فيها من تفصيلات وإيضاحات وأمثلة تطبيقية . وبدون دراستها لا يكتمل للمسلم التعرف إلى أحكام دينه بتمامها كما لا يكتمل للدارس من مسلم أو غيره تصور صحيح شامل لحقيقة الاسلام الحنيف ، وأصوله الروحية والخلقية والتشريعية والحضارية .

وقد لقي القرآن الكريم عناية جيدة من ناحية ترجمة معانيه إلى

اللغة الإنجليزية ، فظهرت حتى الآن عدة ترجمات متفاوتة الصفات ، ولكنها في جملتها تلبي حاجة القارىء إلى فهم النص الأصلي فهماً مرضياً .

أما ترجمة معاني الحديث الشريف ، فإنها لم تكتمل حتى الآن . وما زال باب الجهد في نقلها إلى الإنجليزية بصورة شاملة صحيحة مفتوحاً . وباستثناء بعض الترجمات لمنتخبات من الأحاديث ظهرت في أماكن مختلفة من العالم الإسلامي وخاصة في الباكستان والهند ، فإن أهم جهود الترجمة التي تمت حتى الآن فيما نعلم هي :

١ ـ ترجمة (مشكاة المصابيح) لولي الدين محمد بن عبدالله الخطيب التبريزي المتوفى سنة ٧٣٧ هـ ، قام بها أ. ن.ماثيوز، وظهرت في مجلدين (كلكتا سنتي ١٨٠٩ ، ١٨١٠) وقد نفدت هذه الترجمة منذ زمن بعيد ، وليس من السهل الحصول على نسخة منها . وقد سقطت من هذه الترجمة بعض أحاديث المشكاة .

٢ ـ ترجمة أخرى لـ (مشكاة المصابيح) عنوانها (الحديث) ، قام بها مولانا الحاج فضل الكريم ، وظهرت في أربعة مجلدات (كلكتا سنة ١٩٣٨) مع النص العربي . وقد تصرف المؤلف بعض الشيء في أصل المشكاة ، من حيث تصنيفها ، وأضاف إليها مختارات أخرى من الأحاديث أخذها من (إحياء علوم الدين) للغزالي . ومع ذلك فإن الترجمة تتضمن محتويات (المشكاة) بلا حذف ، وتحتفظ بهيئتها العامة .

٣ ـ جزء من (صحيح البخاري) ، قام بترجمته المسلم النمسوي الأصل محمد أسد ، وظهر مع النص العربي ، (لاهور سنة ١٩٣٨) .

ثم توقف للأسف الشديد .

٤ ـ ترجمة كاملة جديدة لـ (مشكاة المصابيح) ، قام بها الدكتور جيمس روبسون الأستاذ بجامعة مانشستر بإنجلترا ، وظهرت في أربعة أجزاء (لاهور سنة ١٩٦٥) ، وأعيد طبعها سنة ١٩٧٣ .

٥ ـ ترجمة كاملة لـ (صحيح مسلم) ، قام بها عبد الحميد الصدّيقي ، وظهرت في أربعة أجزاء (لاهور ١٩٧٣) .

٦ ـ ترجمة جديدة لـ (صحيح البخاري) ، بدأ بإصدارها باسم الجامعة الإسلامية في المدينة المنورة الدكتور محمد محسن خان ، وستكون هذه الترجمة في أربعة أجزاء ، وتشتمل على النص العربي .

ولا شك أن هذه الجهود جميعاً جديرة بالتقدير الكبير ، كما أنها ـ فيما بينها ـ قد نجحت في نقل قدر جيد من التراث النبوي إلى قراء اللغة الإنجليزية نقلاً مرضياً . إلّا أنه لا يخلو الأمر أحياناً من وجود بعض المآخذ ، إن من ناحية فهم النص العربي فهماً صحيحاً ، وإن من ناحية النقل إلى اللغة الإنجليزية بعبارة مستقيمة مألوفة .

طريقة للترجمة :

وقد أكدت لنا مراجعتنا هذه الترجمات ، ما كنا ندركه دائماً من المشقة التي يتعرض لها المشتغل بترجمة النصوص العربية الدينية إلى اللغة الإنجليزية أو أي لغة أخرى . ذلك أنه يلزم له ، بعد توفيق الله وعونه ، أن يقتدر في ناحيتين باديتي التباعد : إحداهما التمكن من فهم النص العربي عن أصالة طبيعية ومعرفة كافية باللغة العربية والثقافة الإسلامية ، وثانيتهما التمكن في إحكام التعبير الإنجليزي عن أصالة

طبيعية أيضاً في هذه اللغة وتصرف كاف للتعبير بها . وهيهات أن تجتمع هاتان الناحيتان لشخص واحد .

لذلك ، فكرنا في أنه ما لا يجتمع تماماً لشخص واحد ، قد يجتمع لشخصين معاً يعملان متعاونين . ويكون أحدهما عربياً بأصله ، ومسؤولاً عن فهم النص العربي مع دلالاته الدينية ، مع معرفته التامة باللغة الإنجليزية ، بينما يكون الثاني إنجليزي الأصل ومسؤولاً عن سلامة التعبير الإنجليزي وملاءمته للقراءة المعاصرة ، مع معرفته التامة أيضاً باللغة العربية .

وعلى هذا الأساس التقى المترجمان ، وقررا تطبيق هذه الطريقة بالبدء بترجمة مجموعة صغيرة من مختارات الأحاديث النبوية الصحيحة . فإذا قدر لجهودهما أن تنجح ، أمكن الاتجاه إلى ما عدا ذلك من كتب الحديث المطولة .

وقد وقع الاختيار على (متن الأربعين النووية) للإمام يحيى ابن شرف الدين النووي المتوفى سنة ٦٧٦ هـ باكورة لهذا الجهد . باعتبارها واحدة من أشهر المجموعات الصغيرة المعتمدة منذ القرن السابع الهجري حتى الآن ، وكثيراً ما تقرر في المعاهد الدينية لتكون مجموعة البداية لدارسي الحديث الشريف ، نظراً لاشتمالها على أحاديث صحيحة شاملة لأهم أبواب المعرفة الدينية في العقيدة والعبادات والأخلاق والتشريع .

والنية بعد ذلك متجهة إن شاء الله إلى ترجمة معاني مجموعة أخرى من المختارات المتوسطة الطول ، وهي (رياض الصالحين) للإمام النووي نفسه ، وقد يوفق الله تعالى فيستمر الجهد مع مجموعات أخرى في حقل الحديث النبوي الشريف .

أسلوب العمل في هذه الترجمة :

بناء على الطريقة التي اقترحت للترجمة ، تم العمل في هذه المجموعة بالتعاون التام بين المترجمين : منفردين أحياناً ، ومجتمعين معاً غالباً ، ومتضامنين دوماً في إجازة النص الأخير للترجمة .

ومن المفيد أن نشير هنا إلى بعض سمات هذا العمل :

١ ــ عندما احتجت إلى ترجمة معنى آية من القرآن الكريم ، أخذناها من ترجمة الإنجليزي المسلم مارماديوك بكثول المعروفة باسم (معاني القرآن الكريم ــ
The Meaning of the Glorious Koran) .

٢ ــ التزمتْ الترجمة حرفية النص الأصلي ، استهداء بمضمون قوله صلى الله عليه وسلم : « من كذب عليّ عامداً متعمداً ، فليتبوأ مقعده من النار » . وقد اعتبرنا الابتعاد عن حرفية الأصل ضرباً من الافتراء . وعندما أعوز التعبير الإنجليزي إلى تصرف طفيف في هذه الحرفية ، أشرنا الى ذلك صراحة في الهامش ، وحيثما نضطر إلى إضافة كلمة للإيضاح وضعناها بين معقوفين ، لدفع شبهة الافتراق عن الأصل .

٣ ــ هناك كلمات عربية ، لم نستصوب ترجمتها ، إما لكونها اصطلاحاً دينياً مثل (إيمان وإحسان) ، وإما لعدم وجود مقابل دقيق لها في اللغة الإنجليزية مثل (زكاة) ، فأبقيناها بعبارتها العربية .

٤ ــ أسماء الأعلام ، والكلمات العربية التي بقيت على أصلها ، كتبت بالحروف اللاتينية وفقاً لقواعد الـ (transliteration)

المتعارف عليها لدى المشتغلين بالدراسات العربية من غير العرب ، وهي نفس القواعد المتبعة في دائرة المعارف الإسلامية . واستثنيت من ذلك بعض الكلمات المتعارف على كتابتها بشكل خاص في المعاجم الإنجليزية مثل (Caliph) منعاً للَّبْس بلا كبير ضرورة .

٥ ـ آثرنا الاقتصار على الضروري في إيراد الملاحظات الهامشية ، فقللنا عدد الملاحظات واختصرناها ، ولم نورد منها إلا ما لزم لدفع إبهام في النص ، أو إيضاح اصطلاح ، أو إيراد معلومات دينية أو تاريخية تعين على فهم النص ، أو التنبيه على تصرف في الترجمة . ولم نجد داعياً لترجمة شرح النووي للأحاديث اكتفاء باستيعاب هذا الشرح في أثناء ترجمة معاني الأحاديث نفسها .

والله نسأل أن يحقق ما هدفنا إليه من تيسير فهم الأحاديث التي اشتملت عليها هذه المجموعة على القارئين باللغة الإنجليزية ، آملين أن تكون هذه القبسة من التراث النبوي مشجعة لهم على زيادة الاغتراف من هذا المنهل الكريم .

وآخر دعوانا أن الحمد لله رب العالمين .

المترجمان

In the name of Allah the Merciful
the Compassionate

"And take that which the Messenger has brought you".

"Holy Qur'ān"

TRANSLATION OF IMAM AN-NAWAWI'S INTRODUCTION

Praise be to Allah, Lord of the worlds, Eternal Guardian of the heavens and the earths, Disposer of all created beings, Despatcher of Messengers (may the blessings and peace of Allah be upon them all) [who were sent] to those they have been entrusted to guide and to reveal the religious laws to, with positive signs and clear-cut proofs. I praise Him for His favours and ask Him to increase His grace and generosity. I bear witness that there is no god but Allah alone, He having no associate, the One, the Subduer, the Generous, the Pardoner, and I bear witness that our Master Muhammad is His Servant and His Messenger, His dear one and His beloved, the best of created beings, who was honoured with the precious Qur'ān, the enduring miracle through the passing of the years, and with the *sunnas* that enlighten spiritual guides; our Master Muḥammad, singled out for pithiness of speech and tolerance in religion (may the blessings and peace of Allah be upon him, upon the rest of the Prophets and Messengers, and upon all their families and upon the rest of godly persons).

To proceed: It has been transmitted to us on the authority of 'Alī ibn Abī Ṭālib, 'Abdullah ibn Mas'ūd,

بِسْمِ اللَّهِ الرَّحْمَنِ الرَّحِيمِ

﴿ وَمَا آتَاكُمُ الرَّسُولُ فَخُذُوهُ ﴾

« قرآن كريم »

مقدمة الإمام النووي

الحمد لله رب العالمين ، قيوم السموات والأرضين ، مدبر الخلائق أجمعين ، باعث الرسل صلوات الله وسلامه عليهم أجمعين إلى المكلفين ، لهدايتهم وبيان شرائع الدين ، بالدلائل القطعية وواضحات البراهين . أحمده على جميع نعمه وأسأله المزيد من فضله وكرمه . وأشهد أن لا إله إلا الله وحده لا شريك له الواحد القهار ، الكريم الغفار . وأشهد أن سيدنا محمداً عبده ورسوله ، وحبيبه وخليله ، أفضل المخلوقين ، المكرّم بالقرآن العزيز المعجزة المستمرّة على تعاقب السنين ، وبالسنن المستنيرة للمسترشدين ، سيدنا محمد ، المخصوص بجوامع الكلم وسماحة الدين ، صلوات الله وسلامه عليه وعلى سائر النبيين والمرسلين ، وآل كلّ وسائر الصالحين .

أما بعد فقد روينا عن علي بن أبي طالب وعبدالله بن

Muʿādh ibn Jabal, Abū 'd-Dardā', Ibn ʿUmar, Ibn ʿAbbās, Anas ibn Mālik, Abū Huraira and Abū Saʿīd al-Khudrī, (may Allah be pleased with them), through many chains of authorities and in various versions, that the Messenger of Allah (may the blessings and peace of Allah be upon him) said: 'Whosoever memorises and preserves for my People forty Hadith relating to their religion, Allah will resurrect him on the Day of Judgment in the company of jurists and religious scholars'. In another version it reads: 'Allah will resurrect him as a jurist and religious scholar'. In the version of Abū 'd-Dardā' it reads: 'On the Day of Judgment I shall be an intercessor and a witness for him.' In the version of Ibn Masʿūd it reads: 'It will be said to him: Enter by whichever of the doors of Paradise you wish'. In the version of Ibn ʿUmar it reads: 'He will be written down in the company of the religious scholars and will be resurrected in the company of the martyrs'. Scholars of Hadith are agreed that it is a weak Hadith despite its many lines of transmission.

The religious scholars (may Allah be pleased with them) have composed innumerable works in this field. The first one I knew of who did so was ʿAbdullah ibn al-Mubārak, followed by Ibn Aslam aṭ-Ṭūsī, the godly scholar, then al-Ḥasan ibn Sufyān an-Nasāʾī, Abū Bakr al-Ājurrī, Abū Bakr Muḥammad ibn Ibrāhīm al-Aṣfihānī, ad-Dāraquṭnī, al-Ḥākim, Abū Nuʿaim, Abū ʿAbd ar-Raḥmān as-Sulamī, Abū Saʿīd al-Mālīnī, Abū ʿUthmān aṣ-Ṣābūnī, ʿAbdullah ibn Muḥammad al-Anṣārī, Abū Bakr al-Baihaqī, and countless others, both ancient and modern.

I have asked Allah Almighty for guidance in bringing together forty Hadith in emulation of those eminent

مسعود ومعاذ بن جبل وأبي الدرداء وابن عمر وابن عباس وأنس بن مالك وأبي هريرة وأبي سعيد الخدري رضي الله عنهم ، من طرق كثيرات بروايات متنوعة ، أن رسول الله صلى الله عليه وسلم قال : « مَن حفِظ على أمتي أربعين حديثاً من أمر دينها بعثه الله يوم القيامة في زمرة الفقهاء والعلماء ». وفي رواية « بعثه الله فقيهاً عالماً » ، وفي رواية أبي الدرداء « وكنت له يوم القيامة شافعاً وشهيداً » ، وفي رواية ابن مسعود « قيل له : ادخل من أيِّ أبواب الجنة شئْت » ، وفي رواية ابن عمر « كُتِبَ في زمرة العلماء ، وحُشرِ في زمرة الشهداء » . واتفق الحفاظ على أنه حديث ضعيف وإن كثرت طرقه .

وقد صنف العلماء رضي الله عنهم في هذا الباب ما لا يحصى من المصنفات . فأول من علمته صنف فيه عبدالله بن المبارك ، ثم ابن أسلم الطوسي العالم الرَّباني ، ثم الحسن بن سفيان النسائي ، وأبو بكر الآجُري ، وأبو بكر محمد بن إبراهيم الأصفهاني ، والدارقطني ، والحاكم ، وأبو نُعيم ، وأبو عبد الرحمن السُلمي ، وأبو سعيد المالِيني ، وأبو عثمان الصابوني ، وعبدالله بن محمد الأنصاري ، وأبو بكر البيهقي ، وخلائق لا يحصون من المتقدمين والمتأخرين .

وقد استخرت الله تعالى في جمع أربعين حديثاً ، اقتداء

religious leaders and guardians of Islam. Religious scholars are agreed it is permissible to put into practice a weak Hadith if virtuous deeds are concerned; despite this, I do not rely on this Hadith but on his having said (may the blessings and peace of Allah be upon him) the [following] sound Hadith: 'Let him who was a witness among you inform him who was absent', and on his having said (may the blessings and peace of Allah be upon him): 'May Allah make radiant [the face of] someone who has heard what I have said, has learnt it by heart and has transmitted it as he heard it.' Furthermore, there were some religious scholars who brought together forty Hadith on the basic rules of religion, on subsidiary matters, or on *jihād*, while others did so on asceticism, on rules of conduct or on sermons. All these are godly aims—may Allah be pleased with those who pursued them. I, however, considered it best to bring together forty Hadith more important than all of these, being forty Hadith which would incorporate all of these, each Hadith being one of the great precepts of religion, described by religious scholars as being 'the axis of Islam' or 'the half of Islam' or 'the third of it', or the like, and to make it a rule that these forty Hadith be [classified as] sound and that the majority of them be in the Ṣaḥīḥs of al-Bukhārī and Muslim. I give them without the chains of authorities so as to make it easier to memorise them and to make them of wider benefit, if Allah Almighty wills, and I append to them a section explaining abstruse expressions[1].

Every person wishing to attain the Hereafter should know these Hadith because of the important matters

1. The translation has been limited to the text and does not include an-Nawawī's comments.

بهؤلاء الأئمة الأعلام وحفَّاظ الإسلام . وقد اتفق العلماء على جواز العمل بالحديث الضعيف في فضائل الأعمال . ومع هذا فليس اعتمادي على هذا الحديث ، بل على قوله صلى الله عليه وسلم في الأحاديث الصحيحة : « ليبلِّغْ الشاهدُ منكم الغائب » ، وقوله صلى الله عليه وسلم : « نضَّر الله امرأً سمع مقالتي فوعاها فأداها كما سمعها » . ثم من العلماء من جمع الأربعين في أصول الدين ، وبعضهم في الفروع ، وبعضهم في الجهاد ، وبعضهم في الزهد ، وبعضهم في الآداب ، وبعضهم في الخطب ، وكلها مقاصد صالحة رضي الله عن قاصديها . وقد رأيت جمع أربعين أهمَّ من هذا كله . وهي أربعون حديثاً مشتملة ذلك ، وكل حديث منها قاعدة عظيمة من قواعد الدين ، قد وصفه العلماء بأن مدار الإسلام عليه ، أو هو نصف الإسلام أو ثلثه أو نحو ذلك . ثم ألتزم في هذه الأربعين أن تكون صحيحة ، ومعظمها في صحيحي البخاري ومسلم ، وأذكرها محذوفة الأسانيد ليسهل حفظها ويعم الانتفاع بها إن شاء الله تعالى ، ثم أتبعها بباب في ضبط خفيّ ألفاظها .

وينبغي لكل راغب في الآخرة أن يعرف هذه الأحاديث

they contain and the directions they give in respect of all forms of obedience, this being obvious to anyone who has reflected upon it. On Allah do I rely and depend, and to Him do I entrust myself; to Him be praise and grace, and with Him is success and immunity [to error].

* * *

لما اشتملت عليه من المهمات واحتوت عليه من التنبيه على جميع الطاعات ، وذلك ظاهر لمن تدبره . وعلى الله اعتمادي ، وإليه تفويضي واستنادي ، وله الحمد والنعمة ، وبه التوفيق والعصمة .

* * *

HADITH 1

On the authority of the Commander of the Faithful[1], Abū Ḥafṣ 'Umar ibn al-Khaṭṭāb[2] (may Allah be pleased with him), who said: I heard the Messenger of Allah (the blessings and peace of Allah be upon him) say:

> Actions are but by intention and every man shall have but that which he intended. Thus he whose migration[3] was for Allah and His Messenger, his migration was for Allah and His Messenger, and he whose migration was to achieve some worldly benefit or to take some woman in marriage, his migration was for that for which he migrated.

It was related by the two Imāms of the scholars of Hadith, Abū 'Abdullah Muḥammad ibn Ismā·īl ibn Ibrāhīm ibn al-Mughīra ibn Bardizbah al-Bukhārī and Abū 'l-Ḥusain Muslim ibn al-Ḥajjāj ibn Muslim al-Qushairī an-Naisābūrī, in their two Ṣaḥīḥs, which are the soundest of the compiled books[4].

---

1. Title given to the Caliphs.
2. The second Caliph in Islam.
3. This is a reference to religious migration, in particular to that from Mecca to Medina.
4. i.e. collections of Hadith.

الحديث الأول

عَنْ أَمِيرِ الْمُؤْمِنِينَ أَبِي حَفْصٍ عُمَرَ بْنِ الْخَطَّابِ رَضِيَ اللّٰهُ عَنْهُ قَالَ : سَمِعْتُ رَسُولَ اللّٰهِ صَلَّى اللّٰهُ عليه وَسَلَّمَ يَقُولُ :

« إِنَّمَا الْأَعْمَالُ بِالنِّيَّاتِ وَإِنَّمَا لِكُلِّ امْرِئٍ مَا نَوَى ، فَمَنْ كَانَتْ هِجْرَتُهُ إِلَى اللّٰهِ وَرَسُولِهِ فَهِجْرَتُهُ إِلَى اللّٰهِ وَرَسُولِهِ ، وَمَنْ كَانَتْ هِجْرَتُهُ لِدُنْيَا يُصِيبُهَا أَوِ امْرَأَةٍ يَنْكِحُهَا فَهِجْرَتُهُ إِلَى مَا هَاجَرَ إِلَيْهِ . »

رَوَاهُ إِمَامَا الْمُحَدِّثِينَ أَبُو عَبْدِ اللّٰهِ مُحَمَّدُ بْنُ إِسْمَاعِيلَ بْنِ إِبْرَاهِيمَ ابْنِ الْمُغِيرَةِ بْنِ بَرْدِزْبَهْ الْبُخَارِيُّ وَأَبُو الْحُسَيْنِ مُسْلِمُ بْنُ الْحَجَّاجِ بْنِ مُسْلِمٍ الْقُشَيْرِيُّ النَّيْسَابُورِيُّ فِي صَحِيحَيْهِمَا اللَّذَيْنِ هُمَا أَصَحُّ الْكُتُبِ الْمُصَنَّفَةِ .

* * *

HADITH 2

Also on the authority of 'Umar[1] (may Allah be pleased with him), who said:

> One day while we were sitting with the Messenger of Allah (may the blessings and peace of Allah be upon him) there appeared before us a man whose clothes were exceedingly white and whose hair was exceedingly black; no signs of journeying were to be seen on him and none of us knew him. He walked up and sat down by the Prophet (may the blessings and peace of Allah be upon him). Resting his knees against his and placing the palms of his hands on his thighs, he said: O Muḥammad, tell me about Islam. The Messenger of Allah (may the blessings and peace of Allah be upon him) said: Islam is to testify that there is no god but Allah and Muḥammad is the Messenger of Allah, to perform the prayers, to pay the *zakāt*[2], to fast in Ramaḍān, and to make the pilgrimage to the House[3] if

---

1. i.e. 'Umar ibn al-Khaṭṭāb, the second Caliph.
2. Often rendered as "alms-tax" or "poor-due", it is a tax levied on a man's wealth and distributed among the poor.
3. The Ka'ba and Holy Mosque in Mecca.

الحديث الثاني

عَنْ عُمَرَ رَضِيَ اَللَّهُ عَنْهُ أَيْضاً قَالَ :

بَيْنَمَا نَحْنُ جُلُوسٌ عِنْدَ رَسُولِ اَللَّهِ صَلَّى اَللَّهُ عَلَيْهِ وَسَلَّمَ ذَاتَ يَوْمٍ ، إِذْ طَلَعَ عَلَيْنَا رَجُلٌ شَدِيدُ بَيَاضِ الثِّيَابِ ، شَدِيدُ سَوَادِ الشَّعْرِ ، لَا يُرَى عَلَيْهِ أَثَرُ السَّفَرِ ، وَلَا يَعْرِفُهُ مِنَّا أَحَدٌ . حَتَّى جَلَسَ إِلَى النَّبِيِّ صَلَّى اَللَّهُ عَلَيْهِ وَسَلَّمَ . فَأَسْنَدَ رُكْبَتَيْهِ إِلَى رُكْبَتَيْهِ ، وَوَضَعَ كَفَّيْهِ عَلَى فَخِذَيْهِ ، وَقَالَ : يَا مُحَمَّدُ ، أَخْبِرْنِي عَنِ الْإِسْلَامِ . فَقَالَ رَسُولُ اَللَّهِ صَلَّى اَللَّهُ عَلَيْهِ وَسَلَّمَ :«الْإِسْلَامُ أَنْ تَشْهَدَ أَنْ لَا إِلَهَ إِلَّا اَللَّهُ وَأَنَّ مُحَمَّداً رَسُولُ اَللَّهِ ، وَتُقِيمَ اَلصَّلَاةَ ، وَتُؤْتِيَ الزَّكَاةَ ، وَتَصُومَ رَمَضَانَ ، وَتَحُجَّ الْبَيْتَ إِنِ

you are able to do so. He said: You have spoken rightly, and we were amazed at him asking him and saying that he had spoken rightly. He said: Then tell me about *īmān*[4] . He said: It is to believe in Allah, His angels, His books, His messengers, and the Last Day, and to believe in divine destiny, both the good and the evil thereof. He said: You have spoken rightly. He said: Then tell me about *iḥsān*[5]. He said: It is to worship Allah as though you are seeing Him, and while you see Him not yet truly He sees you. He said: Then tell me about the Hour[6] . He said: The one questioned about it knows no better than the questioner. He said: Then tell me about its signs. He said: That the slave-girl will give

---

4. *Īmān* is generally rendered as "religious belief" or "faith". However, being a fundamental term in Islam, the Arabic word has been retained.
5. In this context the word *iḥsān* has a special religious significance and any single rendering of it would be inadequate. Dictionary meanings for *iḥsān* include "right action", "goodness", "charity" , "sincerity", and the like. The root also means "to master or be proficient at" and it is to be found in this meaning in Hadith 17 of the present collection.
6. i.e. of the Day of Judgment.

اسْتَطَعْتَ إِلَيْهِ سَبِيلاً». قَالَ: صَدَقْتَ. فَعَجِبْنَا لَهُ يَسْأَلُهُ وَيُصَدِّقُهُ. قَالَ: فَأَخْبِرْنِي عَنِ الْإِيمَانِ. قَالَ:«أَنْ تُؤْمِنَ بِاللهِ، وَمَلَائِكَتِهِ، وَكُتُبِهِ، وَرُسُلِهِ، وَالْيَوْمِ الْآخِرِ، وَتُؤْمِنَ بِالْقَدَرِ خَيْرِهِ وَشَرِّهِ». قَالَ: صَدَقْتَ. قَالَ: فَأَخْبِرْنِي عَنِ الْإِحْسَانِ. قَالَ: «أَنْ تَعْبُدَ اللهَ كَأَنَّكَ تَرَاهُ، فَإِنْ لَمْ تَكُنْ تَرَاهُ فَإِنَّهُ يَرَاكَ». قَالَ: فَأَخْبِرْنِي عَنِ السَّاعَةِ. قَالَ: «مَا الْمَسْؤُولُ عَنْهَا بِأَعْلَمَ مِنَ السَّائِلِ». قَالَ: فَأَخْبِرْنِي عَنْ أَمَارَاتِهَا قَالَ: «أَنْ تَلِدَ الْأَمَةُ

birth to her mistress[7] and that you will see the barefooted, naked, destitute herdsmen competing in constructing lofty buildings. Then he took himself off and I stayed for a time. Then he said: O 'Umar, do you know who the questioner was? I said: Allah and His Messenger know best. He said: It was Gabriel, who came to you to teach you your religion.

It was related by Muslim.

---

7. This phrase is capable of more than one interpretation. Among those given by an-Nawawī in his commentary is that slave-girls will give birth to sons and daughters who will become free and so be the masters of those who bore them. The word *ama*, normally translated "slave-girl", is also capable of meaning any woman in that we are all slaves or servants of God. The words are thus capable of bearing the meaning: "When a woman will give birth to her master" i.e. a time will come when children will have so little respect for their mothers that they will treat them like servants.

The commentators point out that here the word *rabba* (mistress) includes the masculine *rabb* (master).

رَبَّتَهَا ، وَأَنْ تَرَى الْحُفَاةَ الْعُرَاةَ الْعَالَةَ رِعَاءَ الشَّاءِ يَتَطَاوَلُونَ فِي الْبُنْيَانِ » . ثُمَّ انْطَلَقَ فَلَبِثْتُ مَلِيّاً ثُمَّ قَالَ : « يَا عُمَرُ أَتَدْرِي مَنِ السَّائِلُ ؟ » قُلْتُ : اللهُ وَرَسُولُهُ أَعْلَمُ . قَالَ : « فَإِنَّهُ جِبْرِيلُ أَتَاكُمْ يُعَلِّمُكُمْ دِينَكُمْ » .

رَوَاهُ مُسْلِمٌ .

* * *

HADITH 3

On the authority of Abū 'Abd ar-Raḥmān 'Abdullah, the son of 'Umar ibn al-Khaṭṭāb (may Allah be pleased with them both), who said: I heard the Messenger of Allah (may the blessings and peace of Allah be upon him) say:

Islam has been built on five [pillars][1]: testifying that there is no god but Allah and that Muḥammad is the Messenger of Allah, performing the prayers, paying the *zakāt*[2], making the pilgrimage to the House[3], and fasting in Ramaḍān.

It was related by al-Bukhārī and Muslim.

---

1. The word "pillars" does not appear in the Arabic but has been supplied for clarity of meaning. Pillars (*arkān*) is the generally accepted term in this context.
2. See Note 2 to Hadith 2.
3. See Note 3 to Hadith 2.

الحديث الثالث

عَنْ أَبِي عَبْدِ الرَّحْمْنِ عَبْدِ اللهِ بْنِ عُمَرَ بْنِ الْخَطَّابِ رَضِيَ اللهُ عَنْهُمَا قَالَ : سَمِعْتُ رَسُولَ اللهِ صَلَّى اللهُ عَلَيْهِ وَسَلَّمَ يَقُولُ :

« بُنِيَ الإِسْلَامُ عَلَى خَمْسٍ : شَهَادَةِ أَنْ لَا إِلَهَ إِلَّا اللهُ وَأَنَّ مُحَمَّداً رَسُولُ اللهِ ، وَإِقَامِ الصَّلَاةِ ، وَإِيتَاءِ الزَّكَاةِ ، وَحَجِّ الْبَيْتِ ، وَصَوْمِ رَمَضَانَ » .

رَوَاهُ الْبُخَارِيُّ وَمُسْلِمٌ .

* * *

HADITH 4

On the authority of Abū 'Abd ar-Raḥmān 'Abdullah ibn Mas'ūd (may Allah be pleased with him), who said: The Messenger of Allah (may the blessings and peace of Allah be upon him) and he is the truthful, the believed, narrated to us:

Verily the creation of each one of you is brought together in his mother's belly for forty days in the form of seed, then he is a clot of blood for a like period, then a morsel of flesh for a like period, then there is sent to him the angel who blows the breath of life into him and who is commanded about four matters[1] : to write down his means of livelihood[2] , his life span, his actions, and whether happy or unhappy. By Allah, other than Whom there is no god, verily one of you behaves like the people of Paradise until there is but an arm's length between him and it, and that which has been written overtakes him and so he behaves like the people of Hell-fire and thus he enters it; and one of you behaves like the people of Hell-fire until there is but

1. Lit. "words".
2. The Arabic word *rizq* also possesses such shades of meaning as "daily bread", "fortune", "lot in life", "sustenance provided by Allah", etc.

الحديث الرابع

عَنْ أَبِي عَبْدِ الرَّحْمنِ عَبْدِ اللهِ بْنِ مَسْعُودٍ رضي الله عنْهُ قَالَ : حَدَّثَنَا رَسُولُ اللهِ صَلَّى اللهُ عَلَيْهِ وَسَلَّمَ وَهُوَ الصَّادِقُ الْمَصْدُوقُ :

« إِنَّ أَحَدَكُمْ يُجْمَعُ خَلْقُهُ فِي بَطْنِ أُمِّهِ أَرْبَعِينَ يَوْماً نُطْفَةً ، ثُمَّ يَكُونُ عَلَقَةً مِثْلَ ذَلِكَ ، ثُمَّ يَكُونُ مُضْغَةً مِثْلَ ذَلِكَ ، ثُمَّ يُرْسَلُ إِلَيْهِ الْمَلَكُ فَيَنْفُخُ فِيهِ الرُّوحَ وَيُؤْمَرُ بِأَرْبَعِ كَلِمَاتٍ : بِكَتْبِ رِزْقِهِ ، وَأَجَلِهِ ، وَعَمَلِهِ ، وَشَقِيٌّ أَوْ سَعِيدٌ . فَوَاللهِ الَّذِي لَا إِلَهَ غَيْرُهُ ، إِنَّ أَحَدَكُمْ لَيَعْمَلُ بِعَمَلِ أَهْلِ الْجَنَّةِ ، حَتَّى مَا يَكُونُ بَيْنَهُ وَبَيْنَهَا إِلَّا ذِرَاعٌ ، فَيَسْبِقُ عَلَيْهِ الْكِتَابُ فَيَعْمَلُ بِعَمَلِ أَهْلِ النَّارِ فَيَدْخُلُهَا . وَإِنَّ أَحَدَكُمْ لَيَعْمَلُ بِعَمَلِ أَهْلِ النَّارِ، حَتَّى مَا يَكُونُ

an arm's length between him and it, and that which has been written overtakes him and so he behaves like the people of Paradise and thus he enters it.

It was related by al-Bukhārī and Muslim.

* * *

بَيْنَهُ وَبَيْنَهَا إِلَّا ذِرَاعٌ، فَيَسْبِقُ عَلَيْهِ الْكِتَابُ فَيَعْمَلُ بِعَمَلِ أَهْلِ الْجَنَّةِ فَيَدْخُلُهَا ».

رَوَاهُ الْبُخَارِيُّ وَمُسْلِمٌ.

* * *

HADITH 5

On the authority of the Mother of the Faithful[1], Umm 'Abdullah 'Ā'isha (may Allah be pleased with her), who said: The Messenger of Allah (may the blessings and peace of Allah be upon him) said:

> He who innovates something in this matter of ours that is not of it will have it rejected.

It was related by al-Bukhārī and Muslim. In one version by Muslim it reads:

> He who does an act which our matter is not [in agreement] with will have it rejected.

---

1. A title accorded to any of the Prophet's wives.

الحَدِيثُ الخَامِسُ

عَنْ أُمِّ المُؤْمِنِينَ أُمِّ عَبْدِ اللهِ عَائِشَةَ رَضِيَ اللهُ عَنْهَا قَالَتْ: قَالَ رَسُولُ اللهِ صَلَّى اللهُ عَلَيْهِ وَسَلَّمَ:

« مَنْ أَحْدَثَ فِي أَمْرِنَا هَذَا مَا لَيْسَ مِنْهُ فَهُوَ رَدٌّ ».

رَوَاهُ البُخَارِيُّ وَمُسْلِمٌ وَفِي رِوَايَةٍ لِمُسْلِمٍ:

« مَنْ عَمِلَ عَمَلاً لَيْسَ عَلَيْهِ أَمْرُنَا فَهُوَ رَدٌّ »

* * *

HADITH 6

On the authority of Abū 'Abdullah an-Nu'mān the son of Bashīr (may Allah be pleased with them both), who said: I heard the Messenger of Allah (may the blessings and peace of Allah be upon him) say:

That which is lawful is plain and that which is unlawful is plain and between the two of them are doubtful matters about which not many people know. Thus he who avoids doubtful matters clears himself in regard to his religion and his honour, but he who falls into doubtful matters falls into that which is unlawful, like the shepherd who pastures around a sanctuary, all but grazing therein. Truly every king has a sanctuary, and truly Allah's sanctuary is His prohibitions. Truly in the body there is a morsel of flesh which, if it be whole, all the body is whole and which, if it be diseased, all of it is diseased. Truly it is the heart.

It was related by al-Bukhārī and Muslim.

* * *

الحديث السادس

عَنْ أَبِي عَبْدِ اللهِ النُّعْمَانِ بْنِ بَشِيرٍ رَضِيَ اللهُ عَنْهُمَا قَالَ: سَمِعْتُ رَسُولَ اللهِ صَلَّى اللهُ عَلَيْهِ وَسَلَّمَ يَقُولُ:

« إِنَّ الْحَلَالَ بَيِّنٌ، وَإِنَّ الْحَرَامَ بَيِّنٌ، وَبَيْنَهُمَا أُمُورٌ مُشْتَبِهَاتٌ لَا يَعْلَمُهُنَّ كَثِيرٌ مِنَ النَّاسِ. فَمَنِ اتَّقَى الشُّبُهَاتِ فَقَدِ اسْتَبْرَأَ لِدِينِهِ وَعِرْضِهِ. وَمَنْ وَقَعَ فِي الشُّبُهَاتِ وَقَعَ فِي الْحَرَامِ، كَالرَّاعِي يَرْعَى حَوْلَ الْحِمَى يُوشِكُ أَنْ يَرْتَعَ فِيهِ. أَلَا وَإِنَّ لِكُلِّ مَلِكٍ حِمًى، أَلَا وَإِنَّ حِمَى اللهِ مَحَارِمُهُ. أَلَا وَإِنَّ فِي الْجَسَدِ مُضْغَةً، إِذَا صَلَحَتْ صَلَحَ الْجَسَدُ كُلُّهُ، وَإِذَا فَسَدَتْ فَسَدَ الْجَسَدُ كُلُّهُ، أَلَا وَهِيَ الْقَلْبُ ».

رَوَاهُ الْبُخَارِيُّ وَمُسْلِمٌ.

* * *

HADITH 7

On the authority of Abū Ruqayya Tamīm ibn Aus ad-Dārī (may Allah be pleased with him) that the Prophet (may the blessings and peace of Allah be upon him) said:

> Religion is sincerity![1] We said: To whom? He said: To Allah and His Book, and His Messenger, and to the leaders of the Muslims and their common folk.

It was related by Muslim.

---

1. The Arabic word *naṣīḥa* has a variety of meanings, the most common being "good advice", which is obviously unsuitable in the context. It also gives the meaning of "doing justice to a person or situation", "probity", "integrity", and the like.

الحديث السابع

عَنْ أَبِي رُقَيَّةَ تَمِيمِ بْنِ أَوْسٍ الدَّارِيِّ رَضِيَ اللهُ عَنْهُ أَنَّ النَّبِيَّ صَلَّى اللهُ عَلَيْهِ وَسَلَّمَ قَالَ:

« الدِّينُ النَّصِيحَةُ » قُلْنَا: لِمَنْ؟ قَالَ: « لِلَّهِ، وَلِكِتَابِهِ، وَلِرَسُولِهِ، وَلِأَئِمَّةِ الْمُسْلِمِينَ وَعَامَّتِهِمْ ».

رَوَاهُ مُسْلِمٌ.

* * *

HADITH 8

On the authority of the son of 'Umar[1] (may Allah be pleased with them both) that the Messenger of Allah (may the blessings and peace of Allah be upon him) said:

I have been ordered to fight[2] against people until they testify that there is no god but Allah and that Muhammad is the Messenger of Allah and until they perform the prayers and pay the *zakāt*[3], and if they do so they will have gained protection from me for their lives[4] and property, unless [they do acts that are punishable] in accordance with Islam, and their reckoning will be with Allah the Almighty.

It was related by al-Bukhārī and Muslim.

---

1. See Note 1 to Hadith 2.
2. Islam advocates that conversion be by conviction. The Holy Qur'ān says: "No compulsion in religion", and in another passage the Almighty says: "Call unto the way of thy Lord with wisdom and fair exhortation, and reason with them in the better way". The waging of war is enjoined against certain categories of persons such as those who attack a Muslim country, those who prevent the preaching and spread of Islam by peaceful means, and apostates.
3. See Note 2 to Hadith 2.
4. Lit. "their blood".

الحديث الثامن

عَنِ ابْنِ عُمَرَ رَضِيَ اللهُ عَنْهُمَا أَنَّ رَسُولَ اللهِ صَلَّى اللهُ عَلَيْهِ وَسَلَّمَ قَالَ :

« أُمِرْتُ أَنْ أُقَاتِلَ النَّاسَ حَتَّى يَشْهَدُوا أَنْ لَا إِلَهَ إِلَّا اللهُ وَأَنَّ مُحَمَّداً رَسُولُ اللهِ ، وَيُقِيمُوا الصَّلَاةَ ، وَيُؤْتُوا الزَّكَاةَ . فَإِذَا فَعَلُوا ذَلِكَ عَصَمُوا مِنِّي دِمَاءَهُمْ وَأَمْوَالَهُمْ ، إِلَّا بِحَقِّ الْإِسْلَامِ ، وَحِسَابُهُمْ عَلَى اللهِ تَعَالَى . »

رَوَاهُ الْبُخَارِيُّ وَمُسْلِمٌ .

* * *

HADITH 9

On the authority of Abū Huraira Abd ar-Raḥmān ibn Ṣakhr (may Allah be pleased with him), who said: I heard the Messenger of Allah (may the blessings and peace of Allah be upon him) say:

What I have forbidden to you, avoid; what I have ordered you[to do], do as much of it as you can. It was only their excessive questioning and their disagreeing with their Prophets that destroyed those who were before you.

It was related by al-Bukhārī and Muslim.

* * *

الْحَدِيثُ التَّاسِعُ

عَنْ أَبِي هُرَيْرَةَ عَبْدِ الرَّحْمٰنِ بْنِ صَخْرٍ رَضِيَ اللهُ عَنْهُ قَالَ: سَمِعْتُ رَسُولَ اللهِ صَلَّى اللهُ عَلَيْهِ وَسَلَّمَ يَقُولُ:

« مَا نَهَيْتُكُمْ عَنْهُ فَاجْتَنِبُوهُ، وَمَا أَمَرْتُكُمْ بِهِ فَأْتُوا مِنْهُ مَا اسْتَطَعْتُمْ، فَإِنَّمَا أَهْلَكَ الَّذِينَ مِنْ قَبْلِكُمْ كَثْرَةُ مَسَائِلِهِمْ وَاخْتِلَافُهُمْ عَلَى أَنْبِيَائِهِمْ ».

رَوَاهُ الْبُخَارِيُّ وَمُسْلِمٌ.

* * *

HADITH 10

On the authority of Abū Huraira (may Allah be pleased with him), who said: The Messenger of Allah (may the blessings and peace of Allah be upon him) said:

Allah the Almighty is good and accepts only that which is good. Allah has commanded the Faithful to do that which he commanded the Messengers, and the Almighty has said: **"O ye Messengers! Eat of the good things, and do right."** [1] And Allah the Almighty has said: **"O ye who believe! Eat of the good things wherewith We have provided you."** [2] Then he mentioned [the case of] a man who, having journeyed far, is dishevelled and dusty and who spreads out his hands to the sky [saying]: O Lord! O Lord! – while his food is unlawful, his drink unlawful, his clothing unlawful, and he is nourished unlawfully, so how can he be answered!

It was related by Muslim.

---

1. Qur'ān: verse 51, chapter 23.
2. Qur'ān: verse 172, chapter 2.

الحديث العاشر

عَنْ أَبِي هُرَيْرَةَ رَضِيَ اللهُ عَنْهُ قَالَ : قَالَ رَسُولُ اللهِ صَلَّى اللهُ عَلَيْهِ وَسَلَّمَ :

« إِنَّ اللهَ تَعَالَى طَيِّبٌ لَا يَقْبَلُ إِلَّا طَيِّباً ، وَإِنَّ اللهَ أَمَرَ الْمُؤْمِنِينَ بِمَا أَمَرَ بِهِ الْمُرْسَلِينَ ، فَقَالَ تَعَالَى : ﴿ يَا أَيُّهَا الرُّسُلُ كُلُوا مِنَ الطَّيِّبَاتِ وَاعْمَلُوا صَالِحاً ﴾ وَقَالَ تَعَالَى: ﴿ يَا أَيُّهَا الَّذِينَ آمَنُوا كُلُوا مِنْ طَيِّبَاتِ مَا رَزَقْنَاكُمْ ﴾ ثُمَّ ذَكَرَ الرَّجُلَ يُطِيلُ السَّفَرَ ، أَشْعَثَ أَغْبَرَ ، يَمُدُّ يَدَيْهِ إِلَى السَّمَاءِ : يَا رَبُّ يَا رَبُّ ، وَمَطْعَمُهُ حَرَامٌ ، وَمَشْرَبُهُ حَرَامٌ وَمَلْبَسُهُ حَرَامٌ ، وَغُذِيَ بِالْحَرَامِ ؛ فَأَنَّى يُسْتَجَابُ لَهُ ! » .

رَوَاهُ مُسْلِمٌ .

* * *

HADITH 11

On the authority of Abū Muḥammad al-Ḥasan the son of 'Alī ibn Abī Ṭālib, the grandson of the Messenger of Allah (may the blessings and peace of Allah be upon him) and the one much beloved of him[1] (may Allah be pleased with them both), who said:

I memorised from the Messenger of Allah (may the blessings and peace of Allah be upon him):

> Leave that which makes you doubt for that which does not make you doubt.

It was related by at-Tirmidhī and an-Nasā'ī[2], at-Tirmidhī saying that it was a good and sound Hadith.

---

1. Lit. 'and his fragrant flower'. The word *raiḥāna* was used by the Prophet in respect of al-Ḥasan and al-Ḥusain, the sons of 'Alī ibn Abī Ṭālib, the Prophet's cousin and son-in-law.
2. At-Tirmidhī and an-Nasā'ī were compilers of two of the six recognised collections of Hadith, the other compilers being: al-Bukhārī, Muslim, Abū Dāwūd, and Ibn Mājah.

الحديث الحادي عشر

عَنْ أَبِي مُحَمَّدٍ الْحَسَنِ بْنِ عَلِيِّ بْنِ أَبِي طَالِبٍ سِبْطِ رَسُولِ اللهِ صَلَّى اللهُ عَلَيْهِ وَسَلَّمَ وَرَيْحَانَتِهِ رَضِيَ اللهُ عَنْهُمَا قَالَ : حَفِظْتُ مِنْ رَسُولِ اللهِ صلى الله عليه وسلم :

« دَعْ مَا يَرِيبُكَ إِلَى مَا لَا يَرِيبُكَ » .

رَوَاهُ التِّرْمِذِيُّ وَالنَّسَائِيُّ وَقَالَ التِّرْمِذِيُّ : حَدِيثٌ حَسَنٌ صَحِيحٌ .

* * *

HADITH 12

On the authority of Abū Huraira (may Allah be pleased with him) who said: the Messenger of Allah (may the blessings and peace of Allah be upon him) said:

> Part of someone's being a good Muslim is his leaving alone that which does not concern him.

A good Hadith which was related by at-Tirmidhī and others in this form.

* * *

الحديث الثاني عشر

عَنْ أَبِي هُرَيْرَةَ رَضِيَ اللهُ عَنْهُ قَالَ : قَالَ رَسُولُ اللهِ صَلَّى اللهُ عَلَيْهِ وَسَلَّمَ :

« مِنْ حُسْنِ إِسْلَامِ الْمَرْءِ تَرْكُهُ مَا لَا يَعْنِيهِ » .

حَدِيثٌ حَسَنٌ ، رَوَاهُ التِّرْمِذِيُّ وَغَيْرُهُ هٰكَذَا .

* * *

HADITH 13

On the authority of Abū Hamza Anas ibn Mālik (may Allah be pleased with him), the servant[1] of the Messenger of Allah (may the blessings and peace of Allah be upon him), that the Prophet (may the blessings and peace of Allah be upon him) said:

None of you [truly] believes until he wishes for his brother what he wishes for himself.

It was related by al-Bukhārī and Muslim.

---

1. Anas ibn Mālik, when still a youth, was employed by the Prophet as a servant and is the authority for many Hadith. He is often refered to as "the servant and friend of the Messenger of Allah".

الحديث الثالث عشر

عَنْ أَبِي حَمْزَةَ أَنَسِ بْنِ مَالِكٍ رَضِيَ اللهُ عَنْهُ خَادِمِ رَسُولِ اللهِ صَلَّى اللهُ عَلَيْهِ وَسَلَّمَ، عَنِ النَّبِيِّ صَلَّى اللهُ عَلَيْهِ وَسَلَّمَ قَالَ:

« لَا يُؤْمِنُ أَحَدُكُمْ حَتَّى يُحِبَّ لِأَخِيهِ مَا يُحِبُّ لِنَفْسِهِ ».

رَوَاهُ الْبُخَارِيُّ وَمُسْلِمٌ.

* * *

HADITH 14

On the authority of Ibn Mas'ūd (may Allah be pleased with him), who said: The Messenger of Allah (may the blessings and peace of Allah be upon him) said:

The blood of a Muslim may not be legally spilt other than in one of three [instances]: the married person who commits adultery; a life for a life; and one who forsakes his religion and abandons the community.

It was related by al-Bukhārī and Muslim.

* * *

الحديث الرابع عشر

عَنْ ابْنِ مَسْعُودٍ رَضِيَ اللهُ عَنْهُ قَالَ : قَالَ رَسُولُ اللهِ صَلَّى اللهُ عَلَيْهِ وَسَلَّمَ :

« لَا يَحِلُّ دَمُ امْرِئٍ مُسْلِمٍ إِلَّا بِإِحْدَى ثَلَاثٍ : الثَّيِّبُ الزَّانِي ، وَالنَّفْسُ بِالنَّفْسِ ، وَالتَّارِكُ لِدِينِهِ الْمُفَارِقُ لِلْجَمَاعَةِ » .

رَوَاهُ الْبُخَارِيُّ وَمُسْلِمٌ .

* * *

HADITH 15

On the authority of Abū Huraira (may Allah be pleased with him), that the Messenger of Allah (may the blessings and peace of Allah be upon him) said:

Let him who believes in Allah and the Last Day either speak good or keep silent, and let him who believes in Allah and the Last Day be generous to his neighbour, and let him who believes in Allah and the Last Day be generous to his guest.

It was related by al-Bukhārī and Muslim.

* * *

الحديث الخامس عشر

عَنْ أَبِي هُرَيْرَةَ رَضِيَ اللهُ عَنْهُ أَنَّ رَسُولَ اللهِ صَلَّى اللهُ عَلَيْهِ وَسَلَّمَ قَالَ :

« مَنْ كَانَ يُؤْمِنُ بِاللهِ وَالْيَوْمِ الآخِرِ فَلْيَقُلْ خَيْراً أَوْ لِيَصْمُتْ ، وَمَنْ كَانَ يُؤْمِنُ بِاللهِ وَالْيَوْمِ الآخِرِ فَلْيُكْرِمْ جَارَهُ ، وَمَنْ كَانَ يُؤْمِنُ بِاللهِ وَالْيَوْمِ الآخِرِ فَلْيُكْرِمْ ضَيْفَهُ ».

رَوَاهُ الْبُخَارِيُّ وَمُسْلِمٌ .

* * *

HADITH 16

On the authority of Abū Huraira (may Allah be pleased with him), who said:

A man said to the Prophet (may the blessings and peace of Allah be upon him):

Counsel me. He[1] said: Do not become angry[2]. The man repeated [his request] several times, and he[1] said: Do not become angry.

It was related by al-Bukhārī.

---

1. i.e. the Prophet.
2. An-Nawawī, in his commentary, points out that anger is a natural human trait and that the Hadith is an exhortation not to act when in a state of anger.

الحديث السادس عشر

عَنْ أَبِي هُرَيْرَةَ رَضِيَ اللهُ عَنْهُ:

أَنَّ رَجُلاً قَالَ لِلنَّبِيِّ صَلَّى اللهُ عَلَيْهِ وَسَلَّمَ: أَوْصِنِي، قَالَ: « لَا تَغْضَبْ »، فَرَدَّدَ مِرَاراً، قَالَ: « لَا تَغْضَبْ ».

رَوَاهُ الْبُخَارِيُّ.

* * *

HADITH 17

On the authority of Abū Ya'lā Shaddād ibn Aus (may Allah be pleased with him), that the Messenger of Allah (may the blessings and peace of Allah be upon him) said:

Verily Allah has prescribed proficiency[1] in all things. Thus, if you kill, kill well; and if you slaughter, slaughter well. Let each one of you sharpen his blade and let him spare suffering to the animal he slaughters.

It was related by Muslim.

---

1. See Note 5 to Hadith 2.

الحديث السابع عشر

عَنْ أَبِي يَعْلَى شَدَّادِ بْنِ أَوْسٍ رَضِيَ اللهُ عَنْهُ عَنْ رَسُولِ اللهِ صَلَّى اللهُ عَلَيْهِ وَسَلَّمَ قَالَ:

« إِنَّ اللهَ كَتَبَ الإِحْسَانَ عَلَى كُلِّ شَيْءٍ: فَإِذَا قَتَلْتُمْ فَأَحْسِنُوا الْقِتْلَةَ، وَإِذَا ذَبَحْتُمْ فَأَحْسِنُوا الذِّبْحَةَ، وَلْيُحِدَّ أَحَدُكُمْ شَفْرَتَهُ، وَلْيُرِحْ ذَبِيحَتَهُ ».

* * *

رَوَاهُ مُسْلِمٌ.

HADITH 18

On the authority of Abū Dharr Jundub ibn Junāda and Abū 'Abd ar-Raḥmān Mu'ādh ibn Jabal (may Allah be pleased with them both), that the Messenger of Allah (may the blessings and peace of Allah be upon him) said:

Fear Allah wherever you are, and follow up a bad deed with a good one and it will wipe it out, and behave well towards people.

It was related by at-Tirmidhī, who said it was a good Hadith, and in some copies [of at-Tirmidhī's collection] it was said to be a good and sound Hadith.

* * *

الحَدِيثُ الثَّامِنَ عَشَرَ

عَنْ أَبِي ذَرٍّ جُنْدُبِ بْنِ جُنَادَةَ وَأَبِي عَبْدِ الرَّحْمٰنِ مُعَاذِ بْنِ جَبَلٍ رَضِيَ اللهُ عَنْهُمَا عَنْ رَسُولِ اللهِ صَلَّى اللهُ عَلَيْهِ وَسَلَّمَ قَالَ:

« اتَّقِ اللهَ حَيْثُمَا كُنْتَ، وَأَتْبِعِ السَّيِّئَةَ الْحَسَنَةَ تَمْحُهَا، وَخَالِقِ النَّاسَ بِخُلُقٍ حَسَنٍ ».

رَوَاهُ التِّرْمِذِيُّ وَقَالَ: حَدِيثٌ حَسَنٌ، وَفِي بَعْضِ النُّسَخِ حَسَنٌ صَحِيحٌ.

* * *

HADITH 19

On the authority of Abū 'Abbās 'Abdullah the son of 'Abbās (may Allah be pleased with them both), who said:

One day I was behind[1] the Prophet (may the blessings and peace of Allah be upon him) and he said to me: Young man, I shall teach you some words [of advice]: Be mindful of Allah, and Allah will protect you. Be mindful of Allah, and you will find Him in front of you. If you ask, ask of Allah; if you seek help, seek help of Allah. Know that if the Nation were to gather together to benefit you with anything, it would benefit you only with something that Allah had already prescribed for you, and that if they gather together to harm you with anything, they would harm you only with something Allah had already prescribed for you. The pens have been lifted and the pages have dried.[2]

It was related by at-Tirmidhī, who said it was a good and sound Hadith.

In a version other than that of at-Tirmidhī it reads:

Be mindful of Allah, you will find

---

1. i.e. riding behind him on the same mount.
2. i.e. what has been written and decreed cannot be altered.

الحديث التاسع عشر

عَنْ أَبِي الْعَبَّاسِ عَبْدِ اللهِ بْنِ عَبَّاسٍ رَضِيَ اللهُ عَنْهُمَا قَالَ:

« كُنْتُ خَلْفَ النَّبِيِّ ﷺ يَوْماً فَقَالَ لِي يَا غُلَامُ، إِنِّي أُعَلِّمُكَ كَلِمَاتٍ: اَحْفَظِ اللهَ يَحْفَظْكَ، اَحْفَظِ اللهَ تَجِدْهُ تُجَاهَكَ، إِذَا سَأَلْتَ فَاسْأَلِ اللهَ، وَإِذَا اسْتَعَنْتَ فَاسْتَعِنْ بِاللهِ، وَاعْلَمْ أَنَّ الْأُمَّةَ لَوِ اجْتَمَعَتْ عَلَى أَنْ يَنْفَعُوكَ بِشَيْءٍ لَمْ يَنْفَعُوكَ إِلَّا بِشَيْءٍ قَدْ كَتَبَهُ اللهُ لَكَ، وَإِنِ اجْتَمَعُوا عَلَى أَنْ يَضُرُّوكَ بِشَيْءٍ لَمْ يَضُرُّوكَ إِلَّا بِشَيْءٍ قَدْ كَتَبَهُ اللهُ عَلَيْكَ. رُفِعَتِ الْأَقْلَامُ وَجَفَّتِ الصُّحُفُ ».

رَوَاهُ التِّرْمِذِيُّ وَقَالَ: حَدِيثٌ حَسَنٌ صَحِيحٌ.

وَفِي رِوَايَةِ غَيْرِ التِّرْمِذِيِّ:

« اَحْفَظِ اللهَ تَجِدْهُ أَمَامَكَ، تَعَرَّفْ إِلَى اللهِ

Him before you. Get to know Allah in prosperity and He will know you in adversity. Know that what has passed you by was not going to befall you and that what has befallen you was not going to pass you by. And know that victory comes with patience, relief with affliction, and ease with hardship.

* * *

فِي الرَّخَاءِ يَعْرِفْكَ فِي الشِّدَّةِ ، وَاعْلَمْ أَنَّ مَا أَخْطَأَكَ لَمْ يَكُنْ لِيُصِيبَكَ ، وَمَا أَصَابَكَ لَمْ يَكُنْ لِيُخْطِئَكَ ، وَاعْلَمْ أَنَّ النَّصْرَ مَعَ الصَّبْرِ ، وَأَنَّ الْفَرَجَ مَعَ الْكَرْبِ ، وَأَنَّ مَعَ الْعُسْرِ يُسْراً » .

* * *

HADITH 20

On the authority of Abū Mas'ūd 'Uqba ibn 'Amr al-Anṣārī al-Badrī (may Allah be pleased with him), who said: The Messenger of Allah (may the blessings and peace of Allah be upon him) said:

Among the words people obtained from the First Prophecy[1] are: If you feel no shame, then do as you wish.[2]

It was related by al-Bukhārī.

---

1. i.e. from those Prophets who preceded Muḥammad.
2. This Hadith is recognised as having two possible interpretations: a.) that one may safely act according to one's conscience so long as one feels no shame, and b.) that if one is not capable of any feeling of shame there is nothing to prevent one from behaving as one likes i.e. badly.

الحديث العشرون

عَنْ أَبِي مَسْعُودٍ عُقْبَةَ بْنِ عَمْرٍو الْأَنْصَارِيِّ الْبَدْرِيِّ رضيَ اللهُ عَنْهُ قَالَ: قَالَ رَسُولُ اللهِ صلَّى اللهُ عَلَيْهِ وَسَلَّمَ:

« إِنَّ مِمَّا أَدْرَكَ النَّاسُ مِنْ كَلَامِ النُّبُوَّةِ الْأُولَى: إِذَا لَمْ تَسْتَحِ فَاصْنَعْ مَا شِئْتَ ».

رَوَاهُ الْبُخَارِيُّ.

* * *

HADITH 21

On the authority of Abū 'Amr – and he is also given as Abū 'Amra – Sufyān ibn 'Abdullah (may Allah be pleased with him), who said:

> I said: O Messenger of Allah, tell me something about Islam which I can ask of no one but you. He said: Say: I believe in Allah — and thereafter be upright.

It was related by Muslim.

* * *

الحَدِيثُ الحَادِيَ وَالعِشْرُونَ

عَنْ أَبِي عَمْرٍو - وَقِيلَ أَبِي عَمْرَةَ - سُفْيَانَ بْنِ عَبْدِ اللهِ رَضِيَ اللهُ عَنْهُ قَالَ :

قُلْتُ : يا رَسُولَ اللهِ. قُلْ لِي فِي الإسْلَامِ قَوْلاً لا أَسْأَلُ عَنْهُ أَحَداً غَيْرَكَ ، قال : « قُلْ : آمَنْتُ بِاللهِ ، ثُمَّ اسْتَقِمْ » .

رَوَاهُ مُسْلِمٌ .

* * *

HADITH 22

On the authority of Abū 'Abdullah Jābir the son of 'Abdullah al-Anṣārī (may Allah be pleased with them both):

A man asked the Messenger of Allah (may the blessings and peace of Allah be upon him): Do you think that if I perform the obligatory prayers, fast in Ramaḍān, treat as lawful that which is lawful and treat as forbidden that which is forbidden, and do nothing further, I shall enter Paradise? He said: Yes.

It was related by Muslim.

* * *

الحديث الثاني و العشرون

عَنْ أَبِي عَبْدِ اللهِ جَابِرِ بْنِ عَبْدِ اللهِ الأَنْصَارِيِّ رَضِيَ اللهُ عَنْهُمَا:

أَنَّ رَجُلاً سَأَلَ رَسُولَ اللهِ صَلَّى اللهُ عَلَيْهِ وسَلَّمَ فَقَالَ: أَرَأَيْتَ إِذَا صَلَّيْتُ الْمَكْتُوبَاتِ، وَصُمْتُ رَمَضَانَ، وَأَحْلَلْتُ الْحَلَالَ، وَحَرَّمْتُ الْحَرَامَ، وَلَمْ أَزِدْ عَلَى ذَلِكَ شَيْئاً، أَدْخُلُ الْجَنَّةَ؟ قَالَ: « نَعَمْ ».

رَوَاهُ مُسْلِمٌ.

* * *

HADITH 23

On the authority of Abū Mālik al-Ḥārith ibn 'Āṣim al-Ash'arī (may Allah be pleased with him), who said: The Messenger of Allah (may the blessings and peace of Allah be upon him) said:

> Purity is half of faith. *Al-ḥamdu lillāh* [Praise be to Allah] fills the scales, and *Subḥāna 'llāh* [How far is Allah from every imperfection] and *Al-ḥamdu lillāh* [Praise be to Allah] fill that which is between heaven and earth. Prayer is light; charity is a proof; patience is illumination; and the Qur'ān is an argument for or against you. Everyone starts his day and is a vendor of his soul, either freeing it or bringing about its ruin.

It was related by Muslim.

* * *

اَلْحَدِيثُ الثَّالِثُ وَالْعِشْرُونَ

عَنْ أَبِي مَالِكٍ الْحَارِثِ بْنِ عَاصِمٍ الْأَشْعَرِيِّ رَضِيَ اللهُ عَنْهُ قَالَ: قَالَ رَسُولُ اللهِ صَلَّى اللهُ عَلَيْهِ وَسَلَّمَ:

« اَلطُّهُورُ شَطْرُ الْإِيمَانِ، وَالْحَمْدُ لِلهِ تَمْلَأُ الْمِيزَانَ، وَسُبْحَانَ اللهِ وَالْحَمْدُ لِلهِ تَمْلَآنِ ـ أَوْ تَمْلَأُ ـ مَا بَيْنَ السَّمَاءِ وَالْأَرْضِ، وَالصَّلَاةُ نُورٌ، وَالصَّدَقَةُ بُرْهَانٌ، وَالصَّبْرُ ضِيَاءٌ، وَالْقُرْآنُ حُجَّةٌ لَكَ أَوْ عَلَيْكَ. كُلُّ النَّاسِ يَغْدُو فَبَائِعٌ نَفْسَهُ فَمُعْتِقُهَا أَوْ مُوبِقُهَا. »

رَوَاهُ مُسْلِمٌ.

* * *

HADITH 24

On the authority of Abū Dharr al-Ghifārī (may Allah be pleased with him) from the Prophet (may the blessings and peace of Allah be upon him) is that among the sayings he relates from his Lord[1] (may He be glorified) is that He said:

O My servants, I have forbidden oppression for Myself and have made it forbidden amongst you, so do not oppress one another.

O My servants, all of you are astray except for those I have guided, so seek guidance of Me and I shall guide you. O My servants, all of you are hungry except for those I have fed, so seek food of Me and I shall feed you. O My servants, all of you are naked except for those I have clothed, so seek clothing of Me and I shall clothe you. O My servants, you sin by night and by day, and I forgive all sins, so seek forgiveness of Me and I shall forgive you.

O My servants, you will not attain harming Me so as to harm Me, and you will not attain benefitting Me so as to benefit Me. O My servants, were the

---

[1]. This is a *ḥadīth qudsī* (sacred Hadith) i.e. one in which the Prophet reports what has been revealed to him by Allah, though not necessarily in His actual words. A *ḥadīth qudsī* is in no way regarded as part of the Holy Qur'ān.

الحديث الرابع والعشرون

عَنْ أَبِي ذَرٍّ الغِفَارِيِّ رَضِيَ اللهُ عَنْهُ عَنِ النَّبِيِّ صَلَّى اللهُ عَلَيْهِ وَسَلَّمَ فِيمَا يَرْوِيهِ عَنْ رَبِّهِ عَزَّ وَجَلَّ أَنَّهُ قَالَ:

« يَا عِبَادِي : إِنِّي حَرَّمْتُ الظُّلْمَ عَلَى نَفْسِي وَجَعَلْتُهُ بَيْنَكُمْ مُحَرَّماً فَلَا تَظَالَمُوا.

يَا عِبَادِي : كُلُّكُمْ ضَالٌّ إِلَّا مَنْ هَدَيْتُهُ فَاسْتَهْدُونِي أَهْدِكُمْ. يَا عِبَادِي : كُلُّكُمْ جَائِعٌ إِلَّا مَنْ أَطْعَمْتُهُ فَاسْتَطْعِمُونِي أُطْعِمْكُمْ. يَا عِبَادِي : كُلُّكُمْ عَارٍ إِلَّا مَنْ كَسَوْتُهُ فَاسْتَكْسُونِي أَكْسُكُمْ. يَا عِبَادِي : إِنَّكُمْ تُخْطِئُونَ بِاللَّيْلِ وَالنَّهَارِ، وَأَنَا أَغْفِرُ الذُّنُوبَ جَمِيعاً، فَاسْتَغْفِرُونِي أَغْفِرْ لَكُمْ.

يَا عِبَادِي : إِنَّكُمْ لَنْ تَبْلُغُوا ضُرِّي فَتَضُرُّونِي، وَلَنْ تَبْلُغُوا نَفْعِي فَتَنْفَعُونِي. يَا

first of you and the last of you, the human of you and the jinn of you to be as pious as the most pious heart of any one man of you, that would not increase My kingdom in anything. O My servants, were the first of you and the last of you, the human of you and the jinn of you to be as wicked as the most wicked heart of any one man of you, that would not decrease My kingdom in anything. O My servants, were the first of you and the last of you, the human of you and the jinn of you to rise up in one place and make a request of Me, and were I to give everyone what he requested, that would not decrease what I have, any more than a needle decreases the sea if put into it.[2]

O My servants, it is but your deeds that I reckon up for you and then recompense you for, so let him who finds good[3] praise Allah and let him who finds other than that blame no one but himself.

It was related by Muslim.

---

2. This refers to the minute amount of water adhering to a needle if dipped into the sea and withdrawn.
3. i.e. in the Hereafter.

عِبَادِي : لَوْ أَنَّ أَوَّلَكُمْ وَآخِرَكُمْ وَإِنْسَكُمْ وَجِنَّكُمْ كَانُوا عَلَى أَتْقَى قَلْبِ رَجُلٍ وَاحِدٍ مِنْكُمْ ، مَا زَادَ ذَلِكَ فِي مُلْكِي شَيْئاً . يَا عِبَادِي : لَوْ أَنَّ أَوَّلَكُمْ وَآخِرَكُمْ وَإِنْسَكُمْ وَجِنَّكُمْ كَانُوا عَلَى أَفْجَرِ قَلْبِ رَجُلٍ وَاحِدٍ مِنْكُمْ ، مَا نَقَصَ ذَلِكَ مِنْ مُلْكِي شَيْئاً . يَا عِبَادِي : لَوْ أَنَّ أَوَّلَكُمْ وَآخِرَكُمْ وَإِنْسَكُمْ وَجِنَّكُمْ قَامُوا فِي صَعِيدٍ وَاحِدٍ ، فَسَأَلُونِي ، فَأَعْطَيْتُ كُلَّ وَاحِدٍ مَسْأَلَتَهُ ، مَا نَقَصَ ذَلِكَ مِمَّا عِنْدِي إِلَّا كَمَا يَنْقُصُ الْمِخْيَطُ إِذَا أُدْخِلَ الْبَحْرَ .

يَا عِبَادِي : إِنَّمَا هِيَ أَعْمَالُكُمْ أُحْصِيهَا لَكُمْ ، ثُمَّ أُوَفِّيكُمْ إِيَّاهَا ، فَمَنْ وَجَدَ خَيْراً فَلْيَحْمَدِ اللهَ ، وَمَنْ وَجَدَ غَيْرَ ذَلِكَ فَلَا يَلُومَنَّ إِلَّا نَفْسَهُ » .

رَوَاهُ مُسْلِمٌ .

HADITH 25

Also on the authority of Abū Dharr (may Allah be pleased with him):

Some of the Companions[1] of the Messenger of Allah (may the blessings and peace of Allah be upon him) said to the Prophet (may the blessings and peace of Allah be upon him): O Messenger of Allah, the affluent have made off with the rewards: they pray as we pray, they fast as we fast, and they give away in charity the superfluity of their wealth.

He said: Has not Allah made things for you to give away in charity? Truly every *tasbīḥa*[2] is a charity, every *takbīra*[3] is a charity, every *taḥmīda*[4] is a charity, and every *tahlīla*[5] is a charity; to enjoin a good action is a charity, to forbid an evil action is a charity, and in the sexual act of each of you there is a charity.

They said: O Messenger of Allah, when one of us fulfils his sexual desire

---

1. The Arabic word *Ṣahābī* (pl. *Aṣhāb* or *Ṣahāba*) is given to a person who met the Prophet, believed in him, and died a Muslim.
2. To say *Subḥana 'llāh* (How far is Allah from every imperfection).
3. To say *Allāhu akbar* (Allah is most great).
4. To say *Al-ḥamdu lillāh* (Praise be to Allah).
5. To say *Lā ilāha illā 'llah* (There is no god but Allah).

الْحَدِيثُ الْخَامِسُ وَالْعِشْرُونَ

عَنْ أَبِي ذَرٍّ رَضِيَ اللهُ عَنْهُ أَيْضاً :

أَنَّ نَاساً مِنْ أَصْحَابِ رَسُولِ اللهِ صَلَّى اللهُ عَلَيْهِ وَسَلَّمَ قَالُوا لِلنَّبِيِّ صَلَّى اللهُ تَعَالَى عَلَيْهِ وَسَلَّمَ : يَا رَسُولَ اللهِ ، ذَهَبَ أَهْلُ الدُّثُورِ بِالْأُجُورِ ، يُصَلُّونَ كَمَا نُصَلِّي ، وَيَصُومُونَ كَمَا نَصُومُ ، وَيَتَصَدَّقُونَ بِفُضُولِ أَمْوَالِهِمْ . قَالَ :

« أَوَلَيْسَ قَدْ جَعَلَ اللهُ لَكُمْ مَا تَصَدَّقُونَ ؟ إِنَّ بِكُلِّ تَسْبِيحَةٍ صَدَقَةً ، وَكُلِّ تَكْبِيرَةٍ صَدَقَةً ، وَكُلِّ تَحْمِيدَةٍ صَدَقَةً ، وَكُلِّ تَهْلِيلَةٍ صَدَقَةً ، وَأَمْرٌ بِالْمَعْرُوفِ صَدَقَةٌ ، وَنَهْيٌ عَنْ مُنْكَرٍ صَدَقَةٌ ، وَفِي بُضْعِ أَحَدِكُمْ صَدَقَةٌ » .

قَالُوا : يَا رَسُولَ اللهِ أَيَأْتِي أَحَدُنَا شَهْوَتَهُ

will he have some reward for that? He said: Do you [not] think that were he to act upon it unlawfully he would be sinning? Likewise, if he has acted upon it lawfully he will have a reward.

It was related by Muslim.

* * *

وَيَكُونُ لَهُ فِيها أَجْرٌ؟ قَالَ : « أَرَأَيْتُمْ لَوْ وَضَعَها فِي حَرَامٍ ، أَكَانَ عَلَيْهِ وِزْرٌ ؟ فَكَذَلِكَ إِذَا وَضَعَهَا فِي الْحَلَالِ كَانَ لَهُ أَجْرٌ » .

رَوَاهُ مُسْلِمٌ .

* * *

HADITH 26

On the authority of Abū Huraira (may Allah be pleased with him), who said: The Messenger of Allah (may the blessings and peace of Allah be upon him) said:

Each person's every joint must perform a charity every day the sun comes up: to act justly between two people is a charity; to help a man with his mount, lifting him onto it or hoisting up his belongings onto it is a charity; a good word is a charity; every step you take to prayers[1] is a charity; and removing a harmful thing from the road is a charity.

It was related by al-Bukhārī and Muslim.

---

1. i.e. on your way to the mosque.

الحديث السادس والعشرون

عَنْ أَبِي هُرَيْرَةَ رَضِيَ اللهُ عَنْهُ قَالَ : قَالَ رَسُولُ اللهِ صَلَّى اللهُ عَلَيْهِ وَسَلَّمَ :

« كُلُّ سُلَامَى مِنَ النَّاسِ عَلَيْهِ صَدَقَةٌ كُلَّ يَوْمٍ تَطْلُعُ فِيهِ الشَّمْسُ : تَعْدِلُ بَيْنَ اثْنَيْنِ صَدَقَةٌ ، وَتُعِينُ الرجلَ في دَابَّتِهِ فَتَحْمِلُهُ عَلَيْهَا أَوْ تَرْفَعُ لَهُ عَلَيْهَا مَتَاعَهُ صَدَقَةٌ ، وَالْكَلِمَةُ الطَّيِّبَةُ صَدَقَةٌ ، وَبِكُلِّ خُطْوَةٍ تَمْشِيهَا إِلَى الصَّلَاةِ صَدَقَةٌ ، وَتُمِيطُ الْأَذَى عَنِ الطَّرِيقِ صَدَقَةٌ » .

رَوَاهُ الْبُخَارِيُّ وَمُسْلِمٌ .

* * *

HADITH 27

On the authority of an-Nawwās ibn Samʿān (may Allah be pleased with him) that the Prophet (may the blessings and peace of Allah be upon him) said:

> Righteousness is good morality, and wrongdoing is that which wavers in your soul and which you dislike people finding out about.

It was related by Muslim.

On the authority of Wābiṣa ibn Maʿbad (may Allah be pleased with him), who said:

> I came to the Messenger of Allah (may the blessings and peace of Allah be upon him) and he said: You have come to ask about righteousness? I said: Yes. He said: Consult your heart. Righteousness is that about which the soul feels tranquil and the heart feels tranquil, and wrongdoing is that which wavers in the soul and moves to and fro in the breast even though people again and again have given you their legal opinion [in its favour].[1]

---

[1] The compiler placed these two Hadith together probably because of the similarity of subject matter and phrasing.

الحديث السابع والعشرون

عَنِ النَّوَّاسِ بْنِ سَمْعَانَ رَضِيَ اللهُ عَنْهُ عَنِ النَّبِيِّ صَلَّى اللهُ عَلَيْهِ وَسَلَّمَ قَالَ :

« الْبِرُّ حُسْنُ الْخُلُقِ، وَالْإِثْمُ مَا حَاكَ فِي نَفْسِكَ وَكَرِهْتَ أَنْ يَطَّلِعَ عَلَيْهِ النَّاسُ » .

رَوَاهُ مُسْلِمٌ.

وَعَنْ وَابِصَةَ بْنِ مَعْبَدٍ رَضِيَ اللهُ عَنْهُ قَالَ :

« جِئْتَ تَسْأَلُ عَنِ الْبِرِّ ؟ » قُلْتُ : نَعَمْ. قَالَ : « اِسْتَفْتِ قَلْبَكَ، الْبِرُّ مَا اطْمَأَنَّتْ إِلَيْهِ النَّفْسُ وَاطْمَأَنَّ إِلَيْهِ الْقَلْبُ، وَالْإِثْمُ مَا حَاكَ فِي النَّفْسِ وَتَرَدَّدَ فِي الصَّدْرِ وَإِنْ أَفْتَاكَ النَّاسُ وَأَفْتَوْكَ » .

A good Hadith which we have transmitted from the two Musnads[2] of the two Imāms, Aḥmad ibn Ḥanbal and ad-Dārimī, with a good chain of authorities.

---

2. Collections of Hadith arranged not in accordance with subject matter but under the name of the person who transmitted them from the Prophet.

حَدِيثٌ حَسَنٌ رَوَيْنَاهُ في مُسْنَدَي الإمَامَيْنِ أَحْمَدَ بْنِ حَنْبَلٍ وَالدَّارِمِيِّ بِإِسْنَادٍ حَسَنٍ .

* * *

HADITH 28

On the authority of Abū Najīḥ al-'Irbāḍ ibn Sāriya (may Allah be pleased with him), who said:

> The Messenger of Allah (may the blessings and peace of Allah be upon him) gave us a sermon by which our hearts were filled with fear and tears came to our eyes. We said: O Messenger of Allah, it is as though this is a farewell sermon, so counsel us. He said: I counsel you to fear Allah (may He be glorified) and to give absolute obedience even if a slave becomes your leader. Verily he among you who lives [long] will see great controversy, so you must keep to my *sunna*[1] and to the *sunna* of the rightly-guided Rashidite Caliphs[2] — cling to them stubbornly[3]. Beware of newly invented matters, for every invented matter is an innovation and every innovation is a going astray

---

1. The original meaning of the word is "way" or "path to be followed", but it is used as a technical term for those words, actions and sanctions of the Prophet that were reported and have come down to us.
2. The expression *al-Khulafā' ar-Rāshidūn* is generally translated 'Orthodox Caliphs' but the connotations of the word 'orthodox' render it unsuitable. *Al-Khulafā' ar-Rāshidūn* is the title given to the first four Caliphs in Islam.
3. Lit. "clench your teeth on them".

الحديث الثامن والعشرون

عَنْ أَبِي نَجِيحٍ الْعِرْبَاضِ بْنِ سَارِيَةَ رَضِيَ اللهُ عَنْهُ قَالَ :

وَعَظَنَا رَسُولُ اللهِ صَلَّى اللهُ عَلَيْهِ وَسَلَّمَ مَوْعِظَةً وَجِلَتْ مِنْهَا الْقُلُوبُ، وَذَرَفَتْ مِنْهَا الْعُيُونُ، فَقُلْنَا : يَا رَسُولَ اللهِ، كَأَنَّهَا مَوْعِظَةُ مُوَدِّعٍ، فَأَوْصِنَا. قَالَ : «أُوصِيكُمْ بِتَقْوَى اللهِ عَزَّ وَجَلَّ، وَالسَّمْعِ وَالطَّاعَةِ وَإِنْ تَأَمَّرَ عَلَيْكُمْ عَبْدٌ. فَإِنَّهُ مَنْ يَعِشْ مِنْكُمْ فَسَيَرَى اخْتِلَافًا كَثِيرًا. فَعَلَيْكُمْ بِسُنَّتِي وَسُنَّةِ الْخُلَفَاءِ الرَّاشِدِينَ الْمَهْدِيِّينَ، عَضُّوا عَلَيْهَا بِالنَّوَاجِذِ وَإِيَّاكُمْ وَمُحْدَثَاتِ الْأُمُورِ. فَإِنَّ كُلَّ مُحْدَثَةٍ بِدْعَةٌ وَكُلَّ بِدْعَةٍ ضَلَالَةٌ، وَكُلَّ

and every going astray is in Hell-fire.

It was related by Abū Dāwūd and at-Tirmidhī, who said that it was a good and sound Hadith.

* * *

ضَلالَةٍ فِي النَّارِ ».

رَوَاهُ أَبُو دَاوُدَ وَالتِّرْمِذِيُّ وَقَالَ حَدِيثٌ حَسَنٌ صَحِيحٌ.

* * *

HADITH 29

On the authority of Mu'ādh ibn Jabal (may Allah be pleased with him), who said:

I said: O Messenger of Allah, tell me of an act which will take me into Paradise and will keep me away from Hell-fire. He said: You have asked me about a major matter, yet it is easy for him for whom Allah Almighty makes it easy. You should worship Allah, associating nothing with Him; you should perform the prayers; you should pay the *zakāt*[1]; you should fast in Ramaḍān; and you should make the pilgrimage to the House[2]. Then he said: Shall I not show you the gates of goodness? Fasting [which] is a shield; charity [which] extinguishes sin as water extinguishes fire; and the praying of a man in the depths of night. Then he recited: **"Who forsake their beds to cry unto their Lord in fear and hope, and spend of that We have bestowed on them. No soul knoweth what is kept hid for them of joy, as a reward for what they used to**

---

1. See Note 2 to Hadith 2.
2. See Note 3 to Hadith 2.

الحديث التاسع والعشرون

عَنْ مُعَاذِ بْنِ جَبَلٍ رَضِيَ اللهُ عَنْهُ قَالَ :

قُلْتُ : يَا رَسُولَ اللهِ ، أَخْبِرْنِي بِعَمَلٍ يُدْخِلُنِي الْجَنَّةَ ، وَيُبَاعِدُنِي عَنِ النَّارِ ، قَالَ : «لَقَدْ سَأَلْتَ عَنْ عَظِيمٍ ، وَإِنَّهُ لَيَسِيرٌ عَلَى مَنْ يَسَّرَهُ اللهُ تَعَالَى عَلَيْهِ : تَعْبُدُ اللهَ لَا تُشْرِكُ بِهِ شَيْئاً ، وَتُقِيمُ الصَّلَاةَ ، وَتُؤْتِي الزَّكَاةَ ، وَتَصُومُ رَمَضَانَ ، وَتَحُجُّ الْبَيْتَ . ثُمَّ قَالَ : أَلَا أَدُلُّكَ عَلَى أَبْوَابِ الْخَيْرِ : الصَّوْمُ جُنَّةٌ ، وَالصَّدَقَةُ تُطْفِئُ الْخَطِيئَةَ كَمَا يُطْفِئُ الْمَاءُ النَّارَ ، وَصَلَاةُ الرَّجُلِ فِي جَوْفِ اللَّيْلِ ، ثُمَّ تَلَا : ﴿ تَتَجَافَى جُنُوبُهُمْ عَنِ الْمَضَاجِعِ ﴾ حَتَّى بَلَغَ ﴿ يَعْمَلُونَ ﴾ . ثُمَّ قَالَ :

do[3]." Then he said: Shall I not tell you of the peak of the matter, its pillar, and its topmost part? I said: Yes, O Messenger of Allah. He said: The peak of the matter is Islam; the pillar is prayer; and its topmost part is *jihād*[4]. Then he said: Shall I not tell you of the controlling of all that? I said: Yes, O Messenger of Allah, and he took hold of his tongue and said: Restrain this. I said: O Prophet of Allah, will what we say be held against us? He said: May your mother be bereaved of you, Mu'ādh! Is there anything that topples people on their faces – or he said on their noses – into Hell-fire other than the harvests of their tongues?

It was related by at-Tirmidhī, who said it was a good and sound Hadith.

---

3. Qur'ān: verse 16, chapter 32. In the original Arabic, as is often the practice with a long quotation from the Qur'ān, only the initial words and the final word or words are given.
4. Though the Arabic *jihād* is generally rendered "holy war", its meaning is wider than this and includes any effort made in furtherance of the cause of Islam; it has therefore been decided to retain the Arabic word.

«أَلَا أُخْبِرُكَ بِرَأْسِ الْأَمْرِ وَعَمُودِهِ وَذِرْوَةِ سَنَامِهِ؟»
قُلْتُ: بَلَى يَا رَسُولَ اللهِ. قَالَ: «رَأْسُ الْأَمْرِ الْإِسْلَامُ، وَعَمُودُهُ الصَّلَاةُ، وَذِرْوَةُ سَنَامِهِ الْجِهَادُ».
ثُمَّ قَالَ: «أَلَا أُخْبِرُكَ بِمِلَاكِ ذَلِكَ كُلِّهِ؟».
قُلْتُ: بَلَى يَا رَسُولَ اللهِ، فَأَخَذَ بِلِسَانِهِ وَقَالَ: «كُفَّ عَلَيْكَ هَذَا». قُلْتُ: يَا نَبِيَّ اللهِ، وَإِنَّا لَمُؤَاخَذُونَ بِمَا نَتَكَلَّمُ بِهِ؟ فَقَالَ: «ثَكِلَتْكَ أُمُّكَ يَا مُعَاذُ، وَهَلْ يَكُبُّ النَّاسَ فِي النَّارِ عَلَى وُجُوهِهِمْ ــ أَوْ قَالَ: عَلَى مَنَاخِرِهِمْ ــ إِلَّا حَصَائِدُ أَلْسِنَتِهِمْ؟».

رَوَاهُ التِّرْمِذِيُّ وَقَالَ: حَدِيثٌ حَسَنٌ صَحِيحٌ.

* * *

HADITH 30

On the authority of Abū Thaʻlaba al-Khushanī Jurthūm ibn Nāshir (may Allah be pleased with him) that the Messenger of Allah (may the blessings and peace of Allah be upon him) said:

Allah the Almighty has laid down religious duties, so do not neglect them; He has set boundaries, so do not overstep them; He has prohibited some things, so do not violate them; about some things He was silent—out of compassion for you, not forgetfulness—, so seek not after them.

A good Hadith related by ad-Dāraqutnī and others.

* * *

الْحَدِيثُ الثَّلَاثُونَ

عَنْ أَبِي ثَعْلَبَةَ الْخُشَنِيِّ جُرْثُومِ بْنِ نَاشِرٍ رَضِيَ اللهُ عَنْهُ عَنْ رَسُولِ اللهِ صَلَّى اللهُ عَلَيْهِ وَسَلَّمَ قَالَ:

« إِنَّ اللهَ تَعَالَى فَرَضَ فَرَائِضَ فَلَا تُضَيِّعُوهَا، وَحَدَّ حُدُوداً فَلَا تَعْتَدُوهَا، وَحَرَّمَ أَشْيَاءَ فَلَا تَنْتَهِكُوهَا، وَسَكَتَ عَنْ أَشْيَاءَ رَحْمَةً لَكُمْ غَيْرَ نِسْيَانٍ فَلَا تَبْحَثُوا عَنْهَا ».

حَدِيثٌ حَسَنٌ رَوَاهُ الدَّارَقُطْنِيُّ وَغَيْرُهُ.

* * *

HADITH 31

On the authority of Abū 'l-'Abbās Sahl ibn Sa'd as-Sā'idī (may Allah be pleased with him), who said:

A man came to the Prophet (may the blessings and peace of Allah be upon him) and said: O Messenger of Allah, direct me to an act which, if I do it, [will cause] Allah to love me and people to love me. He said: Renounce the world and Allah will love you, and renounce what people possess and people will love you.

A good Hadith related by Ibn Mājah and others with good chains of authorities.

* * *

الحديث الحادي والثلاثون

عَنْ أَبِي الْعَبَّاسِ سَهْلِ بْنِ سَعْدٍ السَّاعِدِيِّ رَضِيَ اللهُ عَنْهُ قَالَ :

جَاءَ رَجُلٌ إِلَى النَّبِيِّ صَلَّى اللهُ عَلَيْهِ وَسَلَّمَ فَقَالَ : يَا رَسُولَ اللهِ دُلَّنِي عَلَى عَمَلٍ إِذَا عَمِلْتُهُ أَحَبَّنِي اللهُ ، وَأَحَبَّنِي النَّاسُ . فَقَالَ :

« ازْهَدْ فِي الدُّنْيَا يُحِبَّكَ اللهُ ، وَازْهَدْ فِيمَا عِنْدَ النَّاسِ يُحِبَّكَ النَّاسُ » .

رَوَاهُ ابْنُ مَاجَه وَغَيْرُهُ بِأَسَانِيدَ حَسَنَةٍ .

* * *

HADITH 32

On the authority of Abū Saʿīd Saʿd ibn Mālik ibn Sinān al-Khudrī (may Allah be pleased with him) the Messenger of Allah (may the blessings and peace of Allah be upon him) said:

There should be neither harming nor reciprocating harm.

A good Hadith related by Ibn Mājah, ad-Dāraqutnī and others and ranked as *musnad*[1]. It was also related by Mālik in *al-Muwatta*'[2] as *mursal*[3] with a chain of authorities from ʿAmr ibn Yaḥyā, from his father, from the Prophet (may the blessings and peace of Allah be upon him), but leaving out Abū Saʿīd, and he has other chains of authorities that support one another.

---

1. A *musnad* Hadith is one with a complete chain of authorities from the narrator to the Prophet himself.
2. A classic work on Hadith and jurisprudence by Anas ibn Mālik (died 179 A.H.). See Note 1 to Hadith 13.
3. A Hadith that is described as *mursal* is one where the chain of authorities ends with the Follower and does not give the name of the Companion who lies, in the chain, between the Follower and the Prophet himself. The authenticity of a *mursal* Hadith is strengthened if supported by another *mursal* Hadith with a different chain of authorities.
   A Companion, as has been explained in the note to Hadith 25, is a Muslim who had met the Prophet; a Follower *(tābiʿī* pl. *tābiʿūn)* is a Muslim who had met a Companion.

الحَدِيثُ الثَّانِي وَالثَّلَاثُونَ

عَنْ أَبِي سَعِيدٍ سَعْدِ بْنِ مَالِكِ بْنِ سِنَانٍ الْخُدْرِيِّ رَضِيَ اللهُ عَنْهُ أَنَّ رَسُولَ اللهِ صَلَّى اللهُ عَلَيْهِ وَسَلَّمَ قَالَ:

« لَا ضَرَرَ وَلَا ضِرَارَ ».

حَدِيثٌ حَسَنٌ، رَوَاهُ ابْنُ مَاجَه وَالدَّارَقُطْنِيُّ وَغَيْرُهُمَا مُسْنَداً، وَرَوَاهُ مَالِكٌ فِي الْمُوَطَّأ مُرْسَلاً عَنْ عَمْرِو بْنِ يَحْيَى عَنْ أَبِيهِ عَنِ النَّبِيِّ صَلَّى اللهُ عَلَيْهِ وَسَلَّمَ، فَأَسْقَطَ أَبَا سَعِيدٍ. وَلَهُ طُرُقٌ يُقَوِّي بَعْضُهَا بَعْضاً.

* * *

HADITH 33

On the authority of the son of 'Abbās (may Allah be pleased with them both) that the Messenger of Allah (may the blessings and peace of Allah be upon him) said:

> Were people to be given in accordance with their claim, men would claim the fortunes and lives[1] of [other] people, but the onus of proof is on the claimant and the taking of an oath is incumbent upon him who denies.

A good Hadith related by al-Baihaqī and others in this form, and part of it is in the two Ṣaḥīḥs[2].

---

1. Lit. "blood".
2. i.e. the collections of al-Bukhārī and Muslim.

الحديث الثالث والثلاثون

عَنْ ابْنِ عَبَّاسٍ رَضِيَ اللهُ عَنْهُمَا أَنَّ رَسُولَ اللهِ صَلَّى اللهُ عَلَيْهِ وَسَلَّمَ قَالَ :

« لَوْ يُعْطَى النَّاسُ بِدَعْوَاهُمْ، لَادَّعَى رِجَالٌ أَمْوَالَ قَوْمٍ وَدِمَاءَهُمْ ؛ لَكِنِ الْبَيِّنَةُ عَلَى الْمُدَّعِي، وَالْيَمِينُ عَلَى مَنْ أَنْكَرَ » .

حَدِيثٌ حَسَنٌ ، رَوَاهُ الْبَيْهَقِيُّ وَغَيْرُهُ هٰكَذَا وَبَعْضُهُ فِي الصَّحِيحَيْنِ .

* * *

HADITH 34

On the authority of Abū Saʿīd al-Khudrī (may Allah be pleased with him), who said: I heard the Messenger of Allah (may the blessings and peace of Allah be upon him) say:

> Whosoever of you sees an evil action, let him change it with his hand; and if he is not able to do so, then with his tongue; and if he is not able to do so, then with his heart—and that is the weakest of faith.

It was related by Muslim.

* * *

الحديث الرابع والثلاثون

عَنْ أَبِي سَعِيدٍ الْخُدْرِيِّ رَضِيَ اللهُ عَنْهُ قَالَ : سَمِعْتُ رَسُولَ اللهِ صَلَّى اللهُ عَلَيْهِ وَسَلَّمَ يَقُولُ :

« مَنْ رَأَى مِنْكُمْ مُنْكَراً فَلْيُغَيِّرْهُ بِيَدِهِ ، فَإِنْ لَمْ يَسْتَطِعْ فَبِلِسَانِهِ ، فَإِنْ لَمْ يَسْتَطِعْ فَبِقَلْبِهِ ، وَذَلِكَ أَضْعَفُ الْإِيمَانِ » .

رَوَاهُ مُسْلِمٌ .

* * *

HADITH 35

On the authority of Abū Huraira (may Allah be pleased with him), who said: the Messenger of Allah (may the blessings and peace of Allah be upon him) said:

> Do not envy one another; do not inflate prices one to another; do not hate one another; do not turn away from one another; and do no undercut one another, but be you, O servants of Allah, brothers. A Muslim is the brother of a Muslim: he neither oppresses him nor does he fail him, he neither lies to him nor does he hold him in contempt. Piety is right here – and he pointed to his breast three times. It is evil enough for a man to hold his brother Muslim in contempt. The whole of a Muslim for another Muslim is inviolable: his blood, his property, and his honour.

It was related by Muslim.

* * *

الحديث الخامس والثلاثون

عَنْ أَبِي هُرَيْرَةَ رَضِيَ اللهُ عَنْهُ قَالَ : قَالَ رَسُولُ اللهِ صَلَّى اللهُ عَلَيْهِ وَسَلَّمَ :

لَا تَحَاسَدُوا ، وَلَا تَنَاجَشُوا، وَلَا تَبَاغَضُوا ، وَلَا تَدَابَرُوا ، وَلَا يَبِعْ بَعْضُكُمْ عَلَى بَيْعِ بَعْضٍ ، وَكُونُوا ، عِبَادَ اللهِ، إِخْوَاناً. اَلْمُسْلِمُ أَخُو الْمُسْلِمِ : لَا يَظْلِمُهُ ، وَلَا يَخْذُلُهُ ، وَلَا يَكْذِبُهُ ، وَلَا يَحْقِرُهُ . التَّقْوَى هٰهُنَا ـ وَيُشِيرُ إِلَى صَدْرِهِ ثَلَاثَ مَرَّاتٍ ـ بِحَسْبِ امْرِئٍ مِنَ الشَّرِّ أَنْ يَحْقِرَ أَخَاهُ الْمُسْلِمَ . كُلُّ الْمُسْلِمِ عَلَى الْمُسْلِمِ حَرَامٌ : دَمُهُ ، وَمَالُهُ ، وَعِرْضُهُ » .

رَوَاهُ مُسْلِمٌ .

* * *

HADITH 36

On the authority of Abū Huraira (may Allah be pleased with him) that the Prophet (may the blessings and peace of Allah be upon him) said:

Whosoever removes a worldly grief from a believer, Allah will remove from him one of the griefs of the Day of Judgment. Whosoever alleviates [the lot of] a needy person, Allah will alleviate [his lot] in this world and the next. Whosoever shields a Muslim, Allah will shield him in this world and the next. Allah will aid a servant [of His] so long as the servant aids his brother. Whosoever follows a path to seek knowledge therein, Allah will make easy for him a path to Paradise. No people gather together in one of the houses of Allah, reciting the Book of Allah and studying it among themselves, without tranquillity descending upon them, mercy enveloping them, the angels surrounding them, and Allah making mention of them amongst those who are with Him. Whosoever is slowed down[1] by his actions will not be hastened forward by his lineage.

It was related by Muslim in these words.

---

1. i.e. on his path to Paradise.

الحديث السادس والثلاثون

عَنْ أَبِي هُرَيْرَةَ رَضِيَ اللهُ عَنْهُ عَنِ النَّبِيِّ صَلَّى اللهُ عَلَيْهِ وَسَلَّمَ قَالَ :

« مَنْ نَفَّسَ عَنْ مُؤْمِنٍ كُرْبَةً مِنْ كُرَبِ الدُّنْيَا، نَفَّسَ اللهُ عَنْهُ كُرْبَةً مِنْ كُرَبِ يَوْمِ الْقِيَامَةِ. وَمَنْ يَسَّرَ عَلَى مُعْسِرٍ، يَسَّرَ اللهُ عَلَيْهِ فِي الدُّنْيَا وَالْآخِرَةِ. وَمَنْ سَتَرَ مُسْلِماً، سَتَرَهُ اللهُ فِي الدُّنْيَا وَالْآخِرَةِ. وَاللهُ فِي عَوْنِ الْعَبْدِ، مَا كَانَ الْعَبْدُ فِي عَوْنِ أَخِيهِ. وَمَنْ سَلَكَ طَرِيقاً يَلْتَمِسُ فِيهِ عِلْماً، سَهَّلَ اللهُ لَهُ بِهِ طَرِيقاً إِلَى الْجَنَّةِ. وَمَا اجْتَمَعَ قَوْمٌ فِي بَيْتٍ مِنْ بُيُوتِ اللهِ، يَتْلُونَ كِتَابَ اللهِ وَيَتَدَارَسُونَهُ بَيْنَهُمْ، إِلَّا نَزَلَتْ عَلَيْهِمُ السَّكِينَةُ، وَغَشِيَتْهُمُ الرَّحْمَةُ، وَحَفَّتْهُمُ الْمَلَائِكَةُ، وَذَكَرَهُمُ اللهُ فِيمَنْ عِنْدَهُ. وَمَنْ بَطَّأَ بِهِ عَمَلُهُ لَمْ يُسْرِعْ بِهِ نَسَبُهُ ».

رَوَاهُ مُسْلِمٌ بِهَذَا اللَّفْظِ.

* * *

HADITH 37

On the authority of the son of 'Abbās (may Allah be pleased with them both), from the Messenger of Allah (may the blessings and peace of Allah be upon him), is that among the sayings he relates from his Lord (glorified and exalted be He) is that He said:

> Allah has written down the good deeds and the bad ones. Then He explained it [by saying that] he who has intended a good deed and has not done it, Allah writes it down with Himself as a full good deed, but if he has intended it and has done it, Allah writes it down with Himself as from ten good deeds to seven hundred times, or many times over. But if he has intended a bad deed and has not done it, Allah writes it down with Himself as a full good deed, but if he has intended it and has done it, Allah writes it down as one bad deed.

It was related by al-Bukhārī and Muslim in their two Ṣaḥīḥs in these words.

* * *

الحَدِيثُ السَّابِعُ وَالثَّلَاثُونَ

عَنِ ابْنِ عَبَّاسٍ رَضِيَ اللهُ عَنْهُمَا عَنْ رَسُولِ اللهِ صَلَّى اللهُ عَلَيْهِ وَسَلَّمَ فِيمَا يَرْوِيهِ عَنْ رَبِّهِ تَبَارَكَ وَتَعَالَى قَالَ :

« إِنَّ اللهَ كَتَبَ الْحَسَنَاتِ وَالسَّيِّئَاتِ، ثُمَّ بَيَّنَ ذَلِكَ : فَمَنْ هَمَّ بِحَسَنَةٍ فَلَمْ يَعْمَلْهَا كَتَبَهَا اللهُ عِنْدَهُ حَسَنَةً كَامِلَةً ، وَإِنْ هَمَّ بِهَا فَعَمِلَهَا كَتَبَهَا اللهُ عِنْدَهُ عَشْرَ حَسَنَاتٍ إِلَى سَبْعِمَائَةِ ضِعْفٍ إِلَى أَضْعَافٍ كَثِيرَةٍ ، وَإِنْ هَمَّ بِسَيِّئَةٍ فَلَمْ يَعْمَلْهَا كَتَبَهَا اللهُ عِنْدَهُ حَسَنَةً كَامِلَةً ، وَإِنْ هَمَّ بِهَا فَعَمِلَهَا كَتَبَهَا اللهُ سَيِّئَةً وَاحِدَةً . »

رَوَاهُ الْبُخَارِيُّ وَمُسْلِمٌ فِي صَحِيحَيْهِمَا بِهَذِهِ الْحُرُوفِ .

* * *

HADITH 38

On the authority of Abū Huraira (may Allah be pleased with him), who said: the Messenger of Allah (may the blessings and peace of Allah be upon him) said:

Allah the Almighty has said: Whosoever shows enmity to a friend of Mine, I shall be at war with him. My servant does not draw near to Me with anything more loved by Me than the religious duties I have imposed upon him, and My servant continues to draw near to Me with supererogatory works so that I shall love him. When I love him I am his hearing with which he hears, his seeing with which he sees, his hand with which he strikes, and his foot with which he walks. Were he to ask [something] of Me, I would surely give it to him; and were he to ask Me for refuge, I would surely grant him it.

It was related by al-Bukhārī.

* * *

الْحَدِيثُ الثَّامِنُ وَالثَّلَاثُونَ

عَنْ أَبِي هُرَيْرَةَ رَضِيَ اللهُ عَنْهُ قَالَ : قَالَ رَسُولُ اللهِ صَلَّى اللهُ عَلَيْهِ وَسَلَّمَ :

« إِنَّ اللهَ تَعَالَى قَالَ : مَنْ عَادَى لِي وَلِيًّا فَقَدْ آذَنْتُهُ بِالْحَرْبِ . وَمَا تَقَرَّبَ إِلَيَّ عَبْدِي بِشَيْءٍ أَحَبَّ إِلَيَّ مِمَّا افْتَرَضْتُهُ عَلَيْهِ ، وَلَا يَزَالُ عَبْدِي يَتَقَرَّبُ إِلَيَّ بِالنَّوَافِلِ حَتَّى أُحِبَّهُ ؛ فَإِذَا أَحْبَبْتُهُ كُنْتُ سَمْعَهُ الَّذِي يَسْمَعُ بِهِ ، وَبَصَرَهُ الَّذِي يُبْصِرُ بِهِ ، وَيَدَهُ الَّتِي يَبْطِشُ بِهَا ، وَرِجْلَهُ الَّتِي يَمْشِي بِهَا ، وَلَئِنْ سَأَلَنِي لَأُعْطِيَنَّهُ ، وَلَئِنْ اسْتَعَاذَنِي لَأُعِيذَنَّهُ » .

رَوَاهُ الْبُخَارِيُّ .

* * *

HADITH 39

On the authority of the son of 'Abbās (may Allah be pleased with them both) that the Messenger of Allah (may the blessings and peace of Allah be upon him) said:

> Allah has pardoned for me my people for [their] mistakes and [their] forgetfulness and for what they have done under duress.

A good Hadith related by Ibn Mājah, al-Baihaqī, and others.

* * *

الحديث التاسع والثلاثون

عَنْ ابْنِ عَبَّاسٍ رَضِيَ اللهُ عَنْهُمَا أَنَّ رَسُولَ اللهِ صَلَّى اللهُ عَلَيْهِ وَسَلَّمَ قَالَ :

« إِنَّ اللهَ تَجَاوَزَ لِي عَنْ أُمَّتِي الْخَطَأَ ، وَالنِّسْيَانَ ، وَمَا اسْتُكْرِهُوا عَلَيْهِ » .

حَدِيثٌ حَسَنٌ رَوَاهُ ابْنُ مَاجَه وَالْبَيْهَقِيُّ وَغَيْرُهُمَا .

* * *

HADITH 40

On the authority of the son of 'Umar[1] (may Allah be pleased with them both), who said:

The Messenger of Allah (may the blessings and peace of Allah be upon him) took me by the shoulder and said:

Be in the world as though you were a stranger or a wayfarer.

The son of 'Umar[1] (may Allah be pleased with them both) used to say:

At evening do not expect [to live till] morning, and at morning do not expect [to live till] evening. Take from your health for your illness and from your life for your death[2].

It was related by al-Bukhārī.

---

1. See Note 1 to Hadith 2.
2. i.e. while you are in good health you are able to perform your religious duties and should therefore take advantage of this fact. The same applies to the state of being alive.

الحديث الأربعون

عَنْ ابْنِ عُمَرَ رَضِيَ اللهُ عَنْهُمَا قَالَ :

أَخَذَ رَسُولُ اللهِ صَلَّى اللهُ عَلَيْهِ وَسَلَّمَ بِمَنْكِبِي فَقَالَ :

« كُنْ فِي الدُّنْيَا كَأَنَّكَ غَرِيبٌ أَوْ عَابِرُ سَبِيلٍ »

وكَانَ ابْنُ عُمَرَ رَضِيَ اللهُ عَنْهُمَا يَقُولُ :

« إِذَا أَمْسَيْتَ فَلَا تَنْتَظِرِ الصَّبَاحَ ، وَإِذَا أَصْبَحْتَ فَلَا تَنْتَظِرِ الْمَسَاءَ ، وَخُذْ مِنْ صِحَّتِكَ لِمَرَضِكَ وَمِنْ حَيَاتِكَ لِمَوْتِكَ » .

رَوَاهُ الْبُخَارِيُّ .

* * *

HADITH 41

On the authority of Abū Muḥammad 'Abdullah the son of 'Amr ibn al-'Āṣ (may Allah be pleased with them both), who said: The Messenger of Allah (may the blessings and peace of Allah be upon him) said:

None of you [truly] believes until his inclination is in accordance with what I have brought.

A good and sound Hadith which we have transmitted from Kitāb al-Ḥujja[1] with a sound chain of authorities[2].

---

1. The title of a book by Abū 'l-Qāsim Ismā'īl ibn Muḥammad al-Aṣfahānī (died 535 A.H.).

2. The compiler has allowed himself to add two further Hadith to the recognised number of forty, although the title of the work remains "An-Nawawī's Forty".

الْحَدِيثُ الْحَادِي وَالْأَرْبَعُونَ

عَنْ أَبِي مُحَمَّدٍ عَبْدِ اللهِ بْنِ عَمْرِو بْنِ الْعَاصِ رَضِيَ اللهُ عَنْهُمَا قَالَ: قَالَ رَسُولُ اللهِ صَلَّى اللهُ عَلَيْهِ وَسَلَّمَ:

«لَا يُؤْمِنُ أَحَدُكُمْ حَتَّى يَكُونَ هَوَاهُ تَبَعاً لِمَا جِئْتُ بِهِ».

حَدِيثٌ حَسَنٌ صَحِيحٌ رَوَيْنَاهُ فِي كِتَابِ الْحُجَّةِ بِإِسْنَادٍ صَحِيحٍ.

* * *

HADITH 42

On the authority of Anas (may Allah be pleased with him), who said: I heard the Messenger of Allah (may the blessings and peace of Allah be upon him) say:

Allah the Almighty has said: O son of Adam, so long as you call upon Me and ask of Me, I shall forgive you for what you have done, and I shall not mind. O son of Adam, were your sins to reach the clouds of the sky and were you then to ask forgiveness of Me, I would forgive you. O son of Adam, were you to come to Me with sins nearly as great as the earth and were you then to face Me, ascribing no partner to Me, I would bring you forgiveness nearly as great as it[1] .

It was related by at-Tirmidhī, who said that it was a good and sound Hadith.

---

1. i.e. as the earth, meaning that Allah will give forgiveness in like measure to a man's sins.

الحديث الثاني والأربعون

عَنْ أَنَسٍ رَضِيَ اللهُ عَنْهُ قَالَ : سَمِعْتُ رَسُولَ اللهِ صَلَّى اللهُ عَلَيْهِ وَسَلَّمَ يَقُولُ :

« قَالَ اللهُ تَعَالَى: يَا ابْنَ آدَمَ، إِنَّكَ مَا دَعَوْتَنِي وَرَجَوْتَنِي، غَفَرْتُ لَكَ عَلَى مَا كَانَ مِنْكَ وَلَا أُبَالِي. يَا ابْنَ آدَمَ، لَوْ بَلَغَتْ ذُنُوبُكَ عَنَانَ السَّمَاءِ ثُمَّ اسْتَغْفَرْتَنِي، غَفَرْتُ لَكَ. يَا ابْنَ آدَمَ، إِنَّكَ لَوْ أَتَيْتَنِي بِقُرَابِ الْأَرْضِ خَطَايَا ثُمَّ لَقِيتَنِي لَا تُشْرِكُ بِي شَيْئاً، لَأَتَيْتُكَ بِقُرَابِهَا مَغْفِرَةً ».

رَوَاهُ التِّرْمِذِيُّ وَقَالَ حَدِيثٌ حَسَنٌ صَحِيحٌ.

* * *